THE CULTURAL IDIOCY QUIZ

by
RICH DAHM

D1366343

Adams Media Corporation
Holbrook, Massachusetts

For Anne and Madison

—————————

Published by Adams Media Corporation
260 Center Street, Holbrook, MA 02343

ISBN: 1-55850-796-5

Printed in Canada.

J I H G F E D C B A

Cover illustrations by Kurt Dolber.

Interior illlustrations by Dan Vebber on pages 4, 6, 8, 9, 12, 15, 26, 44, 49,
50, 52, 54, 55, 56, 89, 90, 92, 93, 97, 120, 127, 129, 130, 136,
137, 139, 140, 141, 142, 144, 146, 147, 148, 149, 151, 153.

This book is available at quantity discounts for bulk purchases.
For information, call 1-800-872-5627 (in Massachusetts, 781-767-8100).

Visit our home page at http://www.adamsmedia.com

INTRODUCTION

What is Cultural Idiocy?

How much knowledge have you retained from your formal schooling? If you're like most people, not much. A random historical date here, a smattering of a Shakespearean sonnet there, but for the most part, ZILCH!

On the other hand, you can recall the names of all the Pac Man ghosts and sing the Lite-Brite™ jingle without straining a modicum of gray matter.

Some might say this points to a failure in the educational system, but why be negative? Let's celebrate what we've learned from that marvelous invention called modern media. Thanks to the movie, TV, and music industries, our brains house a wealth of information that would be the envy of our ancestors: cartoon catch phrases, movie cast lists, songs about monsters, goofy ad slogans, and so on.

But, you might ask, "Where can I put this effluvia to good use?" Well, the answer is here: <u>The Cultural Idiocy Quiz</u>!

<u>The Cultural Idiocy Quiz</u> lets you mine your cranium for the trivial facts you've been storing all these years. Now you can dazzle your friends with your knowledge of breakfast cereals, sitcoms, and movies starring washed-up sports figures.

Other than a high school history teacher, who cares if you can recite the Gettysburg Address? You'll impress a lot more people if you can sing the theme song to <u>Far Out Space Nuts</u>.

In these media-savvy times, <u>The Cultural Idiocy Quiz</u> shows how smart you really are, focusing on what you know best: pop culture.

Give your ego a boost and take <u>The Cultural Idiocy Quiz</u>.

 # Acknowledgments

I'd like to extend the largest of all possible thank yous to Dan Vebber, who has been my friend and collaborator on many fine projects over the years. Without his help, this book would not exist.

And a big warm kiss on the mouth to Ben Karlin and Scott Dikkers, whose encouragement got this book finished, and Mark Altman for his invaluable advice.

Of course, big thanks to my literary agent Jeff Herman and my editor Ed Walters at Adams Media Corporation for making this book a reality.

I'd also like to extend a hearty thank you to the following people for their support and suggestions over the years: Mark Adams, Ron and Jenny Baird, Christopher Bahn, Caitlin Baldwin, Mark Banker, Molly Bentley, Jenny Braun, Jean Christenson, the Dahm family, John Decker, Joe Garden, Peter Haise, Todd Hanson, Jay Hollenback, Sean LaFleur, John Krewson, Marc and Becky Morehouse, Shaun Mulheron, Matt Nelson, The Onion, Tony Pagel, Troy Parrish, Susan Rathke, the gang at rVision, Maria Schneider, Tony Seaman, the Snyder family, Bryan Tesch, Stephen Thompson, Jun Ueno, Will and Brenda Vervair, Keith Webster, Andrew Welyczko, Christine Wenc and countless others.

And finally, gigantic thanks go to my Mom and Dad and my biggest supporter, my wife, Anne.

Test Your TV IQ!

FRIENDS 4 EVER!

Match the TV characters in the left column with their respective best buddies in the right. Then name the shows they were or are on, or we won't be your friend anymore. So there.

1. "Beaver" Cleaver
2. Lucy Ricardo
3. Kevin Arnold
4. D. J. Tanner
5. Norm Peterson
6. Mike Seaver
7. Dobie Gillis
8. Theo Huxtable
9. Blossom Russo
10. Laverne DeFazio
11. Fred Sanford
12. Patty Greene
13. Chico Rodriguez
14. Ricky Stratton
15. Bart Simpson
16. Kip Wilson
17. Kate McArdle
18. Caroline Duffy
19. Ralph Kramden
20. Mary Richards

A. Henry
B. Ramon
C. Cliff
D. Alfonso
E. Lauren
F. Shirley
G. Maynard
H. Allie
I. Paul
J. Cockroach
K. Ed
L. Rhoda
M. Ethel
N. Annie
O. Larry
P. Kimmy
Q. Grady
R. Six
S. Milhouse
T. Boner

TV SIBS

The following is a list of **TV** brothers and sisters. You must come up with the last name and the **TV** show for each sibling group.

1. Greg, Marcia, Peter, Jan, Bobby, Cindy

2. Sondra, Denise, Theodore, Vanessa, Rudy

3. David, Mary, Joanie, Susan, Nancy, Tommy, Elizabeth, Nicholas

4. John, Jason, Mary Ellen, Ben, Erin, James Robert, Elizabeth

5. Keith, Laurie, Danny, Chris, Tracy

6. Chuck, Richard, Joanie

7. Wallace, Theodore

8. Tabitha, Adam

9. Mike, Robbie, Chip, Ernie

10. J. J., Thelma, Michael

11. Becky, Darlene, D. J., Jerry

12. Mary, Laura, Carrie, Grace

13. Alex, Mallory, Jennifer, Andrew

14. Julie, Barbara

15. Adam, Eric ("Hoss"), Joe

16. Mike, Carol, Ben, Chrissy

17. David, Ricky

18. Quentin, Libby, Patrick

19. Brad, Randy, Mark

20. Betty ("Princess"), Jim Jr. ("Bud"), Kathy ("Kitten")

OH, NO! The baby got into the industrial mucilage, and Mom'll be home any minute!

ANSWERS

1. Brady, *The Brady Bunch*
2. Huxtable, *The Cosby Show*
3. Bradford, *Eight Is Enough*
4. Walton, *The Waltons*
5. Partridge, *The Partridge Family*
6. Cunningham, *Happy Days*
7. Cleaver, *Leave It to Beaver*
8. Stephens, *Bewitched*
9. Douglas, *My Three Sons*
10. Evans, *Good Times*
11. Conner, *Roseanne*
12. Ingalls, *Little House on the Prairie*
13. Keaton, *Family Ties*
14. Cooper, *One Day at a Time*
15. Cartwright, *Bonanza*
16. Seaver, *Growing Pains*
17. Nelson, *The Adventures of Ozzie and Harriet*
18. Kelly, *Grace Under Fire*
19. Taylor, *Home Improvement*
20. Anderson, *Father Knows Best*

You Belong to the City

> **N**ame the U.S. city in which these TV shows were set. Some cities may be fictional.

1. *The Mary Tyler Moore Show*
2. *The Bob Newhart Show*
3. *Cheers*
4. *Welcome Back, Kotter*
5. *Family Ties*
6. *The Andy Griffith Show*
7. *Mork & Mindy*
8. *Designing Women*
9. *Happy Days*
10. *Frasier*
11. *All in the Family*
12. *One Day at a Time*

13. *The Golden Girls*
14. *Hangin' with Mr. Cooper*
15. *Dr. Quinn, Medicine Woman*
16. *Alice*
17. *Hope & Gloria*
18. *Too Close for Comfort*
19. *Quincy*
20. *Scarecrow and Mrs. King*
21. *Dynasty*
22. *Martin*
23. *Hello, Larry*
24. *Eight Is Enough*
25. *I Dream of Jeannie*
26. *The Jeffersons*
27. *The Facts of Life*
28. *Carter Country*
29. *Amen*
30. *Murder, She Wrote*

SPIN-OFF MANIA

Name all the spin-offs for each of the shows listed below. The number in parentheses next to each show indicates the number of spin-offs. Please note that continuations of the original shows, like <u>Archie Bunker's Place</u> and <u>Sanford Arms</u>, and animated versions, are not considered spin-offs here. Also note that #2 contains a spin-off of a spin-off.

1. *Happy Days* (3)

2. *All in the Family* (4)

3. *The Dukes of Hazzard* (1)

4. *Growing Pains* (1)

5. *The Cosby Show* (1)

6. *The Mary Tyler Moore Show* (3)

7. *Soap* (1)

8. *B. J. & the Bear* (1)

9. *Dynasty* (1)

10. *Diff'rent Strokes* (1)

11. *Dallas* (1)

12. *Alice* (1)

13. *Cheers* (2)

14. *Hill Street Blues* (1)

15. *Perfect Strangers* (1)

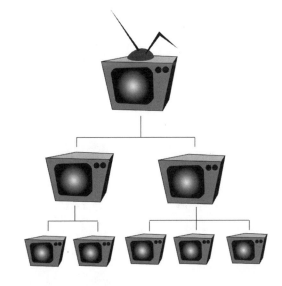

ANSWERS

1. *Laverne and Shirley; Mork and Mindy; Joanie Loves Chachi*

2. *Maude; Good Times* (actually a spin-off of *Maude*); *The Jeffersons; Gloria* (Note: If you remembered *The Jeffersons* spin-off *Checking In* as a spin-off of the Bunker household, but with a different family, give yourself two more points.)

3. *Enos*

4. *Just the Ten of Us*

5. *A Different World*

6. *Rhoda; Phyllis; Lou Grant*

7. *Benson*

8. *The Misadventures of Sheriff Lobo*

9. *The Colbys*

10. *The Facts of Life*

11. *Knot's Landing*

12. *Flo*

13. *The Tortellis; Frasier*

14. *Beverly Hills Buntz*

15. *Family Matters*

A REAL BOSS QUIZ

Match the famous TV boss or superior on the left with the employees on the right. Then name the shows in which they appeared. And be quick about it—time is money!

1. Mr. Spacely
2. Lou Grant
3. Mr. Mooney
4. Oscar Goldman
5. Maxwell Sheffield
6. Capt. James T. Kirk
7. Mr. Slate
8. The Chief
9. Mr. Drysdale
10. Mr. Tudball
11. Alexander Waverly
12. Jimmy James
13. Alan Brady
14. Inspector Fenwick
15. Sgt. Carter
16. Martin Tupper
17. Lt. Martin Castillo
18. Barney Miller
19. Andy Travis
20. Montgomery Burns

YOU'RE FIRED.

A. Jane Hathaway
B. Napoleon Solo, Ilya Kuryakin
C. Dudley Do-Right
D. Robert Petrie
E. Ms. Wiggins
F. Dave Nelson
G. Sonny Crockett, Ricardo Tubbs
H. Homer Simpson
I. Toby Pedalbee
J. Montgomery Scott ("Scotty")
K. George Jetson
L. Stan Wojehowicz
M. Maxwell Smart
N. Mary Richards
O. Johnny Fever
P. Lucy Carmichael
Q. Fran Fine
R. Gomer Pyle
S. Steve Austin
T. Fred Flintstone

Happy Loving Couples

Below are famous dating couples from the magical world of television. Write down the name of the show in which these couples can be seen, then state whether the characters were married during the show's run.

	TV Show	Did they marry?
1. Richie Cunningham and Lori Beth Allen		
2. David Addison and Maddie Hayes		
3. Sam Malone and Diane Chambers		
4. Mork from Ork and Mindy McConnell		
5. Alex Keaton and Ellen Reed		
6. Andy Taylor and Helen Crump		
7. Carmine Ragusa and Shirley Feeney		
8. Maxwell Smart and Agent 99		
9. Tony Nelson and Jeannie		
10. Stephanie Vanderkellen and Michael Harris		
11. Donald Hollinger and Anne Marie		
12. Joe Gerard and Rhoda Morgenstern		
13. Kevin Arnold and Winnie Cooper		
14. Ralph Hinkley and Pam Davidson		
15. Frank Burns and Margaret Houlihan		
16. Martin Payne and Gina Waters		
17. Hayden Fox and Christine Armstrong		
18. Joe Hackett and Helen Chappel		
19. Murphy Brown and Peter Hunt		
20. George Costanza and Susan Biddle Ross		

EVERYONE'S A WINNER

 Name the game shows where you might do the following things:

1. Buy a vowel.
2. Answer questions about your newly acquired spouse.
3. Choose what's behind Door #1, Door #2, or Door #3.
4. Team up with Charles Nelson Reilly to fill in the "blank."
5. Ask "yes" or "no" questions to identify a person's occupation.
6. Identify musical pieces in seven notes or less.
7. Bid closest to the actual retail price without going over.
8. Take Paul Lynde for the block.
9. Provide questions to the Daily Double.
10. Roll dice with Alex Trebek to win big prizes.
11. Get three Xs in row in any direction, and watch out for the dragon.
12. Pull a slot machine lever and avoid the Devil.
13. Identify six categories in an isosceles triangle.
14. Clear the board to solve a rebus.
15. Cooperate with kinfolk to find the most popular answer.
16. Face off against The Gauntlet of Villains.
17. Play blackjack with Wink Martindale.
18. Find out which of three contestants is not lying.
19. Answer a question before the buzzer sounds, or be forced to perform a wacky stunt.
20. Predict whether the value of the next playing card is higher or lower than the one before it.

ANSWERS

1. *Wheel of Fortune*
2. *The Newlywed Game*
3. *Let's Make a Deal*
4. *Match Game*
5. *What's My Line?*
6. *Name That Tune*
7. *The Price Is Right*
8. *The Hollywood Squares*
9. *JEOPARDY!*
10. *High Rollers*
11. *Tic Tac Dough*
12. *The Joker's Wild*
13. *The $10,000 (or $20,000,*
   $25,000, $50,000,
   $100,000) Pyramid
14. *Concentration*
15. *Family Feud*
16. *Whew!*
17. *Gambit*
18. *To Tell the Truth*
19. *Truth or Consequences*
20. *Card Sharks*

SINISTER VILLIANS

Match the famous Saturday-morning villain with his or her goody-two-shoes arch nemesis.

1. Snidely Whiplash
2. Witchiepoo
3. Baron Silas Greenback
4. Zoltar
5. Simon Bar Sinister
6. Crooked Fink
7. Boris and Natasha
8. Dishonest John
9. Benita Bizarre
10. Gargamel
11. Sleestacks
12. Skeletor
13. Savoir Faire
14. Master Cylinder
15. Dr. Claw
16. Sylvester Sneakly
17. The Sea Hag
18. Lotor
19. Tom
20. Mildew Wolf

A. Bullwinkle and Rocky
B. Beany and Cecil
C. Felix the Cat
D. G-Force
E. Inspector Gadget
F. The Smurfs
G. H. R. Pufenstuf
H. He-Man and She-Ra
I. Underdog
J. Dudley Do-Right
K. Danger Mouse
L. Penelope Pitstop
M. Astroboy
N. The Bugaloos
O. The Voltron Force
P. Rick, Will, and Holly Marshall
Q. Klondike Kat
R. Lambsy
S. Jerry
T. Popeye

HAW HAW HAW HAW HAW

Give Us Some Credits!

Following are descriptions of images from the opening credits of various TV shows. Name all the shows, then sing all the theme songs.

1. 3-by-3 grid of smiling faces
2. Cartoon feet tapping to music
3. Stars-and-stripes-covered heart with fireworks in the background
4. Man tripping over ottoman
5. Colorful birds marching in a row
6. Woman flying kite with a caricature of her face on it
7. A fat man and a skinny man steer a boat through a storm.
8. Final image rolls up into a house blueprint
9. Hypnotic spiral spinning against starry background
10. Cartoon family rushing to drive-in theater
11. Man and woman singing "Those Were the Days" at a piano
12. Woman throws hat in air while standing in a busy street
13. Man and boy walk with fishing gear
14. Man and woman in *American Gothic*-like pose
15. Six twenty-somethings frolic in a fountain.
16. Star of show delivers a stand-up comedy bit
17. Celebrity guest stars' faces appear in ship's wheel
18. Man carries boy on shoulders while walking on beach
19. Man disappears through floor of phone booth
20. Giant foot squashes everything

ANSWERS

1. *The Brady Bunch*
2. *My Three Sons*
3. *Love, American Style*
4. *The Dick Van Dyke Show*
5. *The Partridge Family*
6. *That Girl*
7. *Gilligan's Island*
8. *Home Improvement*
9. *The Twilight Zone*
10. *The Flintstones*
11. *All in the Family*
12. *The Mary Tyler Moore Show*
13. *The Andy Griffith Show*
14. *Green Acres*
15. *Friends*
16. *Seinfeld*
17. *The Love Boat*
18. *The Countship of Eddie's Father*
19. *Get Smart*
20. *Monty Python's Flying Circus*

LIVE-ACTION SATURDAY MORNING

Saturday mornings are about more than cartoons. Described below are live-action shows and features that appeared on Saturday mornings during the '70s, '80s, and '90s. Identify them all.

1. Modern family warped to prehistoric times

2. Boy and dragon protected magic flute from witch

3. Man visited fountain of youth; changed into little boy without warning

4. Two boys befriended an unloved sea beast

5. Insect rock band evaded Martha Raye

6. Mad scientist reduced humans to miniature size

7. A man and a woman meted out advice to troubled kids.

8. Boy trapped in land of giant hat people

9. The World's Mightiest Mortal received powers from mythical elders

10. Larry Storch and Forrest Tucker battled ghosts with Tracy the ape.

11. Jim Nabors and Ruth Buzzi were nutty androids.

12. Geeky mad scientist explained science concepts in a wacky way

13. Saturday-morning CBS news segments hosted by Christopher Glenn

14. Mild-mannered science teacher turned into Egyptian goddess

15. Two janitors stranded in space; source of immortal line, "I said *lunch*, not *launch*!"

16. Jason explored outer space with James Doohan

17. Powerhouse female superhero duo battled bad men

18. This faux band rocked *The Krofft Supershow*.

19. Saturday-morning variety show hosted by singing brothers Bill, Brett, and Mark

20. Wrongly accused German shepherd went on the lam, and helped some folks along the way

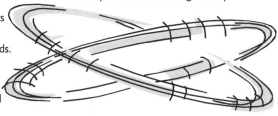

ANSWERS

1. *Land of the Lost*
2. *H. R. Pufnstuf*
3. *Big John, Little John*
4. *Sigmund and the Sea Monsters*
5. *The Bugaloos*
6. *Dr. Shrinker*
7. *Dear Alex and Annie*
8. *Lidsville*
9. *Shazam!*
10. *The Ghost Busters*
11. *The Lost Saucer*
12. *Beakman's World*
13. *In the News*
14. *Isis*
15. *Far Out Space Nuts*
16. *Jason of Star Command*
17. *ElectraWoman and DynaGirl*
18. *Kaptain Kool and the Kongs*
19. *The Hudson Brothers Razzle Dazzle Show*
20. *Run, Joe, Run*

RANDOM TV FACTS, PART 1

Prove your TV mettle. Identify the following:

1. Laverne DeFazio's favorite drink
2. Ricky Ricardo's nightclub
3. Colonel Hogan's first name
4. Richie Cunningham's high school
5. Buddy Sorrell's wife's nickname
6. Favorite waitress of Raj, Rerun, and Duwayne
7. A bathroom sound first heard on *All in the Family*
8. Beaver Cleaver's third-grade teacher
9. Janet DuBois's occupation
10. Samantha Stephens's identical cousin
11. Rhoda's unseen doorman
12. Learning disability that inhibits Donna Martin's progress at school
13. Frequently used sign on Bob Hartley's door
14. Ice skating troupe on *Donny and Marie*
15. Subject taught by Gabriel Kotter

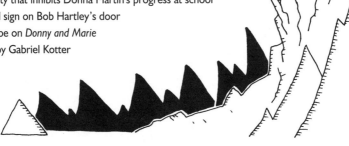

WHAT IS THE MEANING OF LIFE?

Super Fun Puppet Show

Identify these famous puppets (or Muppets or marionettes or ventriloquists' dummies) from their descriptions below.

1. Identify the following Sesame Street Muppets:
   a. Sings about the difficulties of being "green"
   b. Roommate buddies—one loves rubber ducks, the other loves pigeons
   c. Lives in a trash can
   d. Large yellow-feathered nest dweller
   e. Googly-eyed, blue-furred, baked-goods-eater

2. Made it rain ping-pong balls on *Captain Kangaroo*

3. Name the puppet characters from the Neighborhood of Make Believe that live in the following structures:
   a. A clock with no hands
   b. A rocking chair factory
   c. A tree (two answers)
   d. A castle (three answers)
   e. The Museum-Go-Round

4. Chuck's alter ego on *Soap*

5. Pee Wee Herman's ventriloquist dummy

6. Dragon buddy of Kukla and Fran

7. The Peanut Gallery worshipped him

8. "Gnuscaster" on *The Great Space Coaster*

9. Sidekick to ventriloquist Willie Tyler

10. Edgar Bergen's star dummy

11. Bawdy old lady puppet featured in own sitcom

12. Cat-eating orange alien creature

13. Ovine friend of Shari Lewis

SHORT-LIVED TV

Described below are twenty prime time network TV shows that lasted six months or less. Name them all.

1. The only crime drama–musical hybrid to date.
2. Jackie Mason and Lynn Redgrave matched wits and fell in love.
3. David Naughton sang the theme and starred in this disco sitcom.
4. Michelle Pfeiffer played a sorority girl nicknamed "Bombshell."
5. Paul Schaffer and Greg Evigan sold their souls to the Devil to become rock stars.
6. Guest stars had adventures on a luxurious atomic-powered train.
7. Michael Keaton and Jim Belushi were Chicago janitors.
8. Nancy Walker managed a troupe of Las Vegas showgirls.
9. Joe Namath coached a high school basketball team.
10. Variety show hosted by a Japanese singing duo and Jeff Altman.
11. Jeff Goldblum and Ben Vereen were private investigators.
12. A police detective had an unlikely partner— a clumsy robot!
13. Mark Harmon and a Labrador retriever solved crimes.

14. The adventures of the Pittsburgh Pitts, a women's rollerskating team.
15. Richard Benjamin commanded a space garbage scow.
16. Stephen Collins was Nick, Blythe Danner was his ex-wife Hillary, and they ran a restaurant.
17. Gil Girard adopted an Asian orphan, and together they used martial arts to kick butt.
18. A scientist used his power to turn into animals for thwarting evildoers.
19. It shared a name with another new variety show in 1975, but this one was hosted by an infamously verbose sportscaster.
20. Lovable curmudgeon Jack Albertson retired from his professorship to run for the Senate.

ANSWERS

1. Cop Rock
2. Chicken Soup
3. Makin' It
4. Delta House
5. A Year at the Top
6. Supertrain
7. Working Stiffs
8. Blansky's Beauties
9. The Waverly Wonders
10. Pink Lady and Jeff
11. Tenspeed and Brownshoe
12. Holmes and Yoyo
13. Sam
14. Rollergirls
15. Quark
16. Tattinger's (aka Nick and Hillary)
17. Sidekicks
18. Manimal
19. Saturday Night Live with Howard Cosell
20. Grandpa Goes to Washington

SINGLE-MONIKER CRIMEFIGHTERS

Described below are famous TV crimefighter characters whose last names make up the titles of their respective shows. Name them all to earn back your badge. (Remember . . . three answers have two character names in them.)

1. He had a cockatoo named Fred.

2. He sucked lollipops, baby.

3. Peter Falk solved crimes in a rumpled overcoat.

4. He was paralyzed by a gunman's bullet.

5. Dennis Weaver was a marshal in New Mexico.

6. They got the word on the street from Huggy Bear.

7. He was TV's most famous medical examiner.

8. Rotund, mustachioed William Conrad character named for a weapon.

9. John Ritter starred as this "dramedy" detective.

10. Mike Connors played this L.A. private eye.

11. Jameson Parker and Gerald McRaney were mismatched detective brothers.

12. He was a resourceful secret agent who used household items to get out of jams.

13. The TV movie pilot starred Tyne Daly and Loretta Swit, but Sharon Gless replaced Swit on the show.

14. Tom Selleck operated out of a mystery writer's mansion in Hawaii.

15. Retired judge Brian Keith and defendant Daniel Hugh-Kelly dispensed justice.

TV Commonalities

 Find the common bond between the TV shows listed in each group. Be as specific as possible.

1. *My Three Sons*
   The Courtship of Eddie's Father
   Bonanza
   The Andy Griffith Show
   Empty Nest

2. *Hangin' with Mr. Cooper*
   Room 222
   Welcome Back, Kotter
   Head of the Class
   Mr. Rhodes

3. *Bosom Buddies*
   Dave's World
   The Wonder Years
   Get a Life
   Happy Days
   (first two seasons)

4. *The Dick Van Dyke Show*
   Murphy Brown
   The Mary Tyler Moore Show
   Buffalo Bill
   Hope & Gloria

5. *Taxi*
   Matlock
   The Paper Chase
   The Jeff Foxworthy Show
   Sister, Sister

6. *Bewitched*
   I Dream of Jeannie
   Bonanza
   Gunsmoke
   My Three Sons
   The Beverly Hillbillies
   The Andy Griffith Show
   Gilligan's Island
   Dragnet

7. *Barney Miller*
   The Flintstones
   The Andy Griffith Show
   The Simpsons
   All in the Family

8. *Melrose Place*
   Roseanne
   Soap
   Friends
   Ellen

9. *Chico and the Man*
   Cover Up
   Cheers
   Eight Is Enough
   The Royal Family

10. *The Bob Newhart Show*
    Good Times
    Anything But Love
    ER
    Family Matters

11. *Hogan's Heroes*
    Laugh-In
    Match Game
    Family Feud
    Masquerade Party

ANSWERS

1. Shows about widowed fathers
2. Shows about teachers
3. Shows with theme songs that were previously pop songs
4. Shows about fictional TV shows
5. Shows that switched networks
6. Shows that made the transition from black & white to color
7. Shows that feature a recurring character named Barney
8. Shows that made at least one openly gay character
9. Shows in which an actor playing a vital character to the series died
10. Shows set in Chicago
11. Shows that featured Richard Dawson

THE INCREDIBLE TV SPIRAL OF FUN

Starting with #1, name a TV show in which both Gavin MacLeod and Betty White were featured. Continue this pattern for Betty White and Bea Arthur, and the rest of the spiral, until you reach Sherman Hemsley. Then watch TV until your eyes bug out.

Gavin MacLeod
1. _____

Penny Marshall
16. _____

15. _____

Al Molinaro
14. _____

Betty White
2. _____

Ron Howard

Bea Arthur
3. _____

Betty Garrett
17. _____

13. _____

Don Knotts

Isabel Sanford
18. _____

12. _____

Conrad Bain
4. _____

Suzanne Somers

Sherman Hemsley

11. _____

Todd Bridges
5. _____

Patrick Duffy

Abe Vigoda
6. _____

10. _____

Larry Hagman

Hal Linden
7. _____

Suzanne Pleshette
8. _____

9. _____

Bill Daily

MORE RANDOM TV FACTS

Prove your TV mettle. Identify the following:

1. Barney Miller's precinct number
2. The teenage singing group on *The Electric Company*
3. Movie producer that visited *Gilligan's Island*
4. First of the *Facts of Life* girls to lose her virginity
5. The singer of *The Dukes of Hazzard* theme song
6. Henry Rush's wardrobe of choice
7. Elise Keaton's occupation
8. The title of the *Schoolhouse Rock* segment about pronouns
9. Buffy Davis's ever-present doll
10. First five cities to experience *The Real World*
11. ALF's home planet
12. Count Floyd's horror movie show on *SCTV*
13. Jaime Sommers's bionic parts
14. The word Johnny Fever uttered on air that got him fired from the station he worked at before WKRP
15. The first names of Oscar Madison's and Felix Unger's ex-wives

ANSWERS

1. 12
2. The Short Circus
3. Harold Hecuba, played by Phil Silvers
4. Natalie
5. Waylon Jennings
6. College sweatshirts
7. Architect
8. Rufus Xavier Sarsaparilla
9. Mrs. Beasley
10. New York, Los Angeles, San Francisco, London, Miami
11. Melmac
12. *Monster Chiller Horror Theater*
13. Legs, right ear, right arm
14. Booger
15. Oscar's wife was Blanche, Felix's was Gloria

Variety Pack

On what TV variety shows might you have seen these sights?

1. Mr. Bill, a land shark, and Killer Bees

2. A plate-spinning guy, Señor Wences, and the Beatles

3. A woman claiming to be "a little bit country"; her brother replying that he's "a little bit rock 'n' roll"

4. The host tugging her ear while singing the closing theme

5. Pat Paulsen running for president and Pete Seeger singing a Vietnam protest song

6. Husband insulting wife's nose; wife insulting husband's lack of height

7. Geraldine exclaiming, "What you see is what you get!"

8. People popping their heads out of small doors to tell jokes and Goldie Hawn wearing body paint

9. Sid Caesar, Rob Reiner, and Imogene Coca yukking it up

10. The boozy host flirting with the Golddiggers

11. Freddie the Freeloader and Clem Kadiddlehopper

12. A tough clown, a disabled superhero, and "Men on Film"

13. Husband-and-wife mimes acting like robots

14. An animated donkey in a straw hat and Roy Clark

15. A bear telling jokes, a juggler throwing fish, and some pigs in outer space

16. Stupid pet tricks, Melman Bus Lines, and elevator races

17. A former TV family sharing the spotlight with synchronized swimmers

Now it's time for a little of the ol' soft shoe...

ANSWERS

1. Saturday Night Live
2. The Ed Sullivan Show
3. Donny and Marie
4. The Carol Burnett Show
5. The Smothers Brothers
6. The Sonny and Cher Comedy Hour
7. The Flip Wilson Show
8. Laugh-In
9. Your Show of Shows
10. The Dean Martin Show
11. The Red Skelton Show
12. In Living Color
13. Shields and Yarnell
14. Hee Haw
15. The Muppet Show
16. Late Night with David Letterman
17. The Brady Bunch Hour

SERVANTS' QUARTERS

Like most American homes, TV households are brimming with maids, butlers, and other hired help. Identify the characters described below, then name their shows. Or, if you don't feel like it, order your butler to do it.

1. George and Louise Jefferson's maid
2. Mike and Carol Brady's maid
3. George and Dorothy Baxter's maid
4. Jonathan and Jennifer Hart's chauffeur
5. Philip Drummond's first housekeeper
6. Maxwell Sheffield's butler
7. Bruce Wayne's butler
8. Danny Williams's maid
9. Jack Benny's valet
10. Chester and Jessica Tate's two butlers
11. Tom Corbett's housekeeper
12. Ben Cartwright's cook
13. Angela Bower's housekeeper
14. Oliver Douglas's farmhand
15. Gomez Addams's butler
16. Philip and Vivian Banks' butler
17. Bill Davis's manservant
18. George and Marsha Owens' housekeeper
19. Carl Kanisky's housekeeper
20. David Tucker and Jay Bostwick's maid

RANDOM TV FACTS, PART 3

Impress friends, family, and clergy with your grasp of TV trivia. Identify the following:

1. The Clampetts' term for the swimming pool
2. Theme song to *Cops*
3. Legendary creature battled by Steve Austin in a two-part episode of *The Six Million Dollar Man*
4. The faux rock band that visited *Gilligan's Island*
5. Clarence Rutherford's nickname on *Leave It to Beaver*
6. The Munsters' address
7. The host of *The Battle of the Network Stars*
8. Murphy Brown's TV show
9. Greg, Marsha, Jan, and Peter's junior high school
10. Sister Bertrille's convent
11. Mork's schizophrenic pal
12. The full name of *The Love Boat*'s Gopher
13. Elaine Nardo's aspiration (beyond taxi driving)
14. Couple that got married on *The Tonight Show*
15. Ratio of men to women in a typical game of *Studs*
16. How George Jefferson alleviated Bentley's back pain
17. The Shakespearean play spoofed in full costume on *Moonlighting*
18. Nickname for Hawkeye and Trapper John's tent
19. The name of the evil spirit on *Twin Peaks*
20. What you do when someone says the secret word on *Pee Wee's Playhouse*

Working for a Living

Even TV characters have to put food on the table. On the left is a list of twenty TV workplaces, on the right twenty TV character employees. Match them up, then just for kicks, name the shows they were featured in. And have this done by the 9:30 meeting or you're fired!

1. McKenzie, Brackman, Chaney & Kuzak
2. St. Eligius
3. Sugarbaker's
4. McMahon & Tate
5. Mel's Diner
6. Sunshine Cab Company
7. Charles Townshend Associates
8. Office of Strategic Information
9. Independent News Service
10. Wellman Plastics
11. Crossroads Bus Terminal
12. Connors & Davenport
13. Long Branch Saloon
14. Blue Moon Detective Agency
15. *The Sacramento Register*
16. J. Peterman
17. St. Gregory Hotel
18. *The Los Angeles Tribune*
19. *The Pacific Princess*
20. Shady Rest Hotel

A. Kitty Russell
B. Sabrina Duncan
C. Dennis "Animal" Price
D. Tom Bradford
E. Carl Kolchak
F. Darrin Stephens
G. Ann Romano
H. Elaine Benes
I. Isaac Washington
J. Mark Craig
K. Mary Jo Shively
L. Christine Francis
M. Agnes Dipesto
N. Arnie Becker
O. Alice Hyatt
P. Roseanne Conner
Q. Kate Bradley
R. Steve Austin
S. John Hemingway
T. Alex Reiger

BIG SCREEN, LITTLE SCREEN

Name the actor who was featured in all three of the movies listed in each of the twenty groups below. Big Fat Hint: All twenty actors were (or are) stars of hit TV shows.

1. Doc Hollywood; Light of Day; Casualties of War

2. Same Time, Next Year; Crimes & Misdemeanors; Whispers in the Dark

3. Divorce American Style; Dick Tracy; Chitty Chitty Bang Bang

4. Hero at Large; Skin Deep; Problem Child

5. The Brass Bottle; Chattanooga Choo Choo; Harper Valley P.T.A.

6. The Devil and Max Devlin; Mother, Jugs, and Speed; California Suite

7. Rollercoaster; The Waterdance; Twister

8. Catch-22; On a Clear Day You Can See Forever; First Family

9. The Sure Thing; Gotcha; Mr. North

10. Mame; Sorrowful Jones; Yours, Mine, & Ours

11. Three Men and a Baby; Pontiac Moon; Body Heat

12. The In-Laws; Wings of Desire; The Cheap Detective

13. L.A. Story; Excalibur; Jeffrey

14. A Face in the Crowd; No Time for Sergeants; Rustler's Rhapsody

15. The Hollywood Knights; Going Ape!; She's Out of Control

16. Little Big Man; S.O.B.; Teachers

17. Beethoven; Don't Tell Mom the Babysitter's Dead; Kalifornia

18. Kelly's Heroes; The Dirty Dozen; Go-Bots: Battle of the Rock Lords

19. Change of Habit; Ordinary People; Flirting with Disaster

20. Pillow Talk; Seven Faces of Dr. Lao; Hello Down There

ANSWERS

1. Michael J. Fox
2. Alan Alda
3. Dick Van Dyke
4. John Ritter
5. Barbara Eden
6. Bill Cosby
7. Helen Hunt
8. Bob Newhart
9. Anthony Edwards
10. Lucille Ball
11. Ted Danson
12. Peter Falk
13. Patrick Stewart
14. Andy Griffith
15. Tony Danza
16. Richard Mulligan
17. David Duchovny
18. Telly Savalas
19. Mary Tyler Moore
20. Tony Randall

RANDOM CARTOON FACTS

Test your cartoon capabilities. Identify the following:

1. Underdog's girlfriend
2. Hometown of Fat Albert
3. Uncle Scrooge's last name
4. Nell Fenwick's true love
5. Mr. Magoo's nephew
6. Foghorn Leghorn's favorite song
7. Color of Huckleberry Hound's fur
8. Danger Mouse's sidekick
9. Three teams of the Laff-A-Lympics
10. First Tom and Jerry cartoon
11. Where Hong Kong Phooey kept the Phooeymobile
12. Boris and Natasha's superior
13. Cereal named after the Smurfs
14. Instrument played by Veronica of The Archies
15. Popeye's nephews
16. Kangaroo mistaken for a mouse by Sylvester and Sylvester, Jr.
17. Voice of Woody Woodpecker
18. What Yukk, of Mighty Man and Yukk, wore on his head
19. What "Eep Opp Ork Ah Ah" meant
20. The "artist" who disrupted Daffy's life in *Duck Amuck*

160 **BAZILLION TONS**

Medical Professionals

Described below are twenty TV shows about medical professionals. Name them all, then treat yourself to a sponge bath.

1. Starred Robert Young, the guy from the Sanka commercials

2. A child prodigy became a doctor

3. Its final episode suggested the series was all part of an autistic boy's imagination.

4. This frontier woman is not only a doctor, but a willing adopter of orphans.

5. Unlikely *M*A*S*H* spin-off featuring a character named Gonzo

6. Sitcom starred Matt Frewer, TV's *Max Headroom*

7. TV version of a Walter Matthau–Art Carney movie

8. Show that made Chad Everett a star

9. Starred Richard Chamberlain before he became king of the miniseries

10. Short-lived sitcom starred Paul Lynde and Cleavon Little

11. This animated psychologist has mostly stand-up comics for patients.

12. Randy Mantooth and Kevin Tighe played paramedics Gage and Desoto.

13. A New York doctor lived amongst Alaskan town folks.

14. Stars one of the main nerds from *Revenge of the Nerds*, and was created by the guy who wrote *Jurassic Park*

15. Starred the guy who played Inigo Montoya from *The Princess Bride*

16. Miracle–working neurosurgeon played by Vince Edwards

17. An obstetrician and his lawyer wife raised their kids in Brooklyn

18. A psychiatrist and his journalist wife raised their kids on Long Island

19. Extremely short-lived Elliott Gould sitcom from the mid-80s

20. A pediatrician lived with his adult daughters and big dog.

> As your doctor, I prescribe... MORE TV WATCHING!

CARTOON ANALOGIES

⭐ You say you have trouble with the analogy sections on standardized tests? That's because the subjects of the relationships are unfamiliar things. Now, if they had analogies about cartoons, you'd ace 'em. Well, this is your lucky day. Complete the cartoon analogies below by coming up with the best answers to complete the relationships. Then state what the relationship is between the two parts.

Ex. Bugs Bunny is to carrot as Scooby Doo is to _____.
    Answer: Scooby Snack; favorite foods

1. Spinach is to Popeye as _____ is to Underdog.

2. Mr. Twiddle is to Wally Gator as _____ is to Tennessee Tuxedo.

3. Nancy is to Sluggo as Little Lulu is to _____.

4. Fred Flintstone is to "Yabba Dabba Doo!" as Fat Albert is to _____.

5. Casey Kasem is to Shaggy as _____ is to The Great Gazoo.

6. Dudley Do-Right is to the Canadian Mounties as Danger Mouse is to _____.

7. Heckle is to Jeckle as Pixie is to _____.

8. Peter Potamus is to his Magic Flying Balloon as Mr. Peabody is to _____.

9. Cholly is to Mr. Magoo as _____ is to Richie Rich.

10. Yogi Bear is to Jellystone Park as Casper is to _____.

11. Astro is to the Jetsons as _____ is to the Roman Holidays.

12. The Road Runner is to Wile E. Coyote as Foghorn Leghorn is to _____.

Sci-Fi TV Primer

Sci-fi geeks will ace this quiz, but for the rest of us, here's a few brain twisters that test your knowledge of science fiction TV. Answer them all.

1. Name the only original *Star Trek* episode in which Spock smiled.
2. What did TARDIS stand for in *Dr. Who*?
3. How many episodes of the original *Twilight Zone* featured living ventriloquist dummies?
4. Name the space colony on *Space: 1999*.
5. How long each day could the Gemini Man be invisible?
6. Name the annoying robot on *Buck Rogers in the 25th Century*.
7. If Richard Hatch was Apollo and Dirk Benedict was Starbuck, who was Maren Jensen?
8. What disaster movie maven created *Lost in Space* and *Land of the Giants*?
9. Name the top secret agency that monitored the skies in *UFO*.
10. The characters in *Sliders* travel to different dimensions in the same city. Name the city.
11. Who was the first real historical figure Sam Beckett inhabited in *Quantum Leap*?
12. "We will control the horizontal. We will control the vertical," opened this sci-fi anthology.
13. This Patrick Duffy series was the first American TV show aired in China.
14. Name the friendly talking dolphin in *Seaquest DSV*.
15. Who played Deanna Troi's mother on *Star Trek: The Next Generation*?

ANSWERS

1. "Amok Time"
2. Time and Relative Dimensions in Space
3. Two. "The Dummy" with Cliff Robertson and "Caesar and Me" with Jackie Cooper.
4. Moonbase Alpha
5. Fifteen minutes
6. Twiki
7. Athena (from *Battlestar Galactica*)
8. Irwin Allen
9. SHADO (Supreme Headquarters, Alien Defense Organization)
10. San Francisco
11. Lee Harvey Oswald
12. *The Outer Limits*
13. *The Man from Atlantis*
14. Darwin
15. Majel Barrett, who played Nurse Chapel on the original *Star Trek*, and also happened to be creator Gene Roddenberry's wife.

HOLLY JOLLY CHRISTMAS

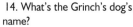

❄ ❄ ❄ Answer these holiday special trivia questions. ❄ ❄ ❄

1. In *Santa Claus Is Coming to Town*, what does the Winter Warlock give to Kris Kringle to make reindeer fly?

2. What causes Frosty the Snowman to melt?

3. What's the main course at the Whoville Christmas feast?

4. In *Rudolph the Red-Nosed Reindeer*, what is Mrs. Claus' main concern regarding Santa?

5. Which of these is NOT on the Island of Misfit Toys: a Charlie-in-the-Box, a water pistol that shoots jelly, a bird that swims, a cowboy riding an ostrich, a boat that can't stay afloat, or a choo-choo train with square wheels?

6. What makes Happy a "misfit" in *Rudolph's Shiny New Year*?

7. What carol do the children sing at the end of *A Charlie Brown Christmas*?

8. Where does Marge Simpson hide her jar of Christmas money?

9. How did Nestor the Long-Eared Donkey's mother die?

10. What do the kids wish for in *A Family Circus Christmas*, and do they get it?

11. In *The Year Without a Santa Claus*, name the two brothers who control the weather.

12. What does Frosty say every time the hat is put back on his head?

13. Who's the man who hates toys in *Santa Claus Is Coming to Town*?

14. What's the Grinch's dog's name?

15. When Yukon Cornelius and the Abominable Snow Monster fall from a cliff, why aren't they killed?

16. In *T'was The Night Before Christmas*, who nearly sabotages Christmas by not believing in Santa?

Kids...please answer them all correctly or we'll have to cancel Christmas!

ANSWERS

1. Magical corn
2. He gets locked in a greenhouse by Professor Hinkle.
3. Roast beast
4. She's worried he won't be fat enough for Christmas.
5. Trick question. They all live there.
6. He has big ears.
7. "Hark the Herald Angels Sing"
8. In her hair
9. She freezes to death protecting her son from the icy chill of winter.
10. They wish for a visit from their dead grandfather.
11. Heatmiser and Snowmiser
12. "Happy Birthday"
13. Burgermeister Meisterburger
14. Max
15. In Cornelius's words, "Bumbles bounce."
16. Albert Mouse

HOSTS WITH THE MOST

Listed below are twenty TV shows with hosts or narrators. Name the people who originally hosted these shows when they first aired, or we'll make you wait in the Green Room.

1. *That's Incredible*
2. *Real People*
3. *In Search Of . . .*
4. *Those Amazing Animals*
5. *Mutual of Omaha's Wild Kingdom*
6. *America's Funniest Home Videos*
7. *60 Minutes*
8. *That's Hollywood*
9. *The Love Connection*
10. *Ripley's Believe It or Not*
11. *Rescue 911*
12. *Unsolved Mysteries*
13. *America's Most Wanted*
14. *Candid Camera*
15. *ABC's Wide World of Sports*
16. *Dance Fever*
17. *The Today Show*
18. *Masterpiece Theater*
19. *Tomorrow*
20. *The Tonight Show*

My first guest tonight is a can of common house paint...

The HOST Show

Spelling Bee

God bless Aaron Spelling, the greatest producer in the history of television. Practically everything his name is associated with has turned to gold. Identify the Aaron Spelling shows from the premises described below and judge for yourself.

1. Three buxom women were hired as detectives by an unseen boss.
2. California high school teens cope with problems, changing fashions, and Shannen Doherty.
3. A violent cop show with a catchy theme and an acronym title.
4. A cruise ship for out-of-work actors staffed by a future Iowa congressman and Gavin MacLeod.
5. Twenty-somethings like Heather Locklear and Andrew Shue live and love in L.A.
6. The guy who sang "Don't Give Up On Us Baby" and the guy who directed *Cop and a Half* were cops who drove around in a red car with a white stripe.
7. A mysterious man and his dwarf assistant helped people live out their dreams.
8. Serious drama featuring Kristy McNichol and Meredith Baxter when she was still a Birney.
9. A wealthy husband and wife with a gravelly-voiced chauffeur solved crimes just for kicks.
10. A fancy hotel admitted has-been actors while Dr. Welby's assistant and John Tesh's future wife looked on.
11. Private eye Dan Tanna solved crimes in the gambling capital.
12. Three fresh-faced police recruits, one of whom was Michael Ontkean, fought crimes.
13. Three hippie stereotypes—"one white, one black, one blond"—were undercover cops.
14. Suzanne Pleshette headed a phalanx of nurses who wore very little.

PRIME-TIME IMAGE MAKEOVERS

Some **TV** stars aren't content with just one hit show. The characters described in the left column were played by an actor who later played one of the characters described in the right column. Match the former role with the latter, then name the actors and the respective **TV** shows.

1. Small town sheriff
2. Psychiatrist
3. Wife of comedy writer
4. Millionaire hillbilly
5. Astronaut
6. Tennis instructor/spy
7. Keyboard player in family singing group
8. Sloppy sportswriter
9. Liberal housewife
10. Las Vegas private eye
11. Wacky judge
12. Bigoted loading dock worker
13. Owner of dry-cleaning chain
14. Hardware store owner
15. Bionic man
16. Criminal lawyer
17. Old West card shark
18. Boxer/cab driver
19. Caretaker of talking car
20. Boarding school girl

Randy Scofield as "That Hopkins Boy"

Randy Scofield in "Memphis Vice"

A. Medical examiner
B. Widowed housekeeper
C. Author/hotel owner/TV host
D. Assistant DA
E. TV news associate producer
F. Mississippi police chief
G. Head lifeguard
H. Wheelchair-bound detective
I. Man-hungry socialite
J. Boston private eye
K. Priest
L. Church deacon
M. Semi-retired private eye
N. Atlanta attorney
O. Syndicated newspaper columnist
P. Obstetrician
Q. Malibu ex-con private eye
R. Conniving oil tycoon
S. Divorced teacher
T. Hollywood stuntman

ANSWERS

1. N, Andy Griffith (The Andy Griffith Show, Matlock)
2. C, Bob Newhart (The Bob Newhart Show, Newhart)
3. E, Mary Tyler Moore (The Dick Van Dyke Show, The Mary Tyler Moore Show)
4. M, Buddy Ebsen (The Beverly Hillbillies, Barnaby Jones)
5. R, Larry Hagman (I Dream of Jeannie, Dallas)
6. F, Bill Cosby (I Spy, The Cosby Show)
7. D, Susan Dey (The Partridge Family, L.A. Law)
8. A, Jack Klugman (The Odd Couple, Quincy)
9. S, Bea Arthur (Maude, The Golden Girls)
10. J, Robert Urich (Vegas, Spenser: For Hire)
11. O, Harry Anderson (Night Court, Dave's World)
12. F, Carroll O'Connor (All in the Family, In the Heat of the Night)
13. L, Sherman Hemsley (The Jeffersons, Amen)
14. K, Tom Bosley (Happy Days, Father Dowling Mysteries)
15. T, Lee Majors (The Six Million Dollar Man, The Fall Guy)
16. H, Raymond Burr (Perry Mason, Ironside)
17. Q, James Garner (Maverick, The Rockford Files)
18. B, Tony Danza (Taxi, Who's The Boss?)
19. G, David Hasselhoff (Knight Rider, Baywatch)
20. I, Kim Fields (The Facts of Life, Living Single)

LET IT ALL HANGOUT

Name the TV shows in which these hangouts appear, then go to Frank's Place for a delicious bowl of gumbo.

1. The Peach Pit
2. Pizza Bowl
3. Regal Beagle
4. Arnold's
5. Central Perk
6. Phil's Place
7. Riff's
8. The Brick
9. Rob's
10. Hooper's Store
11. Kelsey's
12. Moe's
13. Monk's Cafe
14. Mario's
15. The Minute Man Cafe
16. Pop's Chocklit Shoppe
17. Double R Diner
18. Remo's
19. Buy the Book
20. Ten Forward

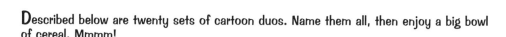

Cartoon Chums

Described below are twenty sets of cartoon duos. Name them all, then enjoy a big bowl of cereal. Mmmm!

1. A moose and a squirrel
2. Two identical magpies
3. Two chipmunks, one with a big red nose
4. A penguin and a walrus
5. A green clay man and a horse
6. A horse and a burro
7. A boy and a sea serpent
8. An orange canine and his son
9. A Chihuahua and a fat cat
10. A rabbit and a coyote
11. A teenage werewolf and his cousin
12. A hippopotamus and a monkey
13. A lion and a hyena
14. A squirrel and a mole
15. A rabbit and a tiger
16. A shark with a German accent and a catfish
17. A turtle and a big shaggy dog
18. A lion monarch and a skunk
19. A polar bear and a seal
20. A human superhero and a robotic dog

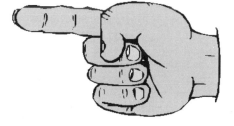

FIXING A HOLE

When important characters are written out of TV shows due to an actor's death or contract expiration, new characters must be brought in to fill the gap. Below are some such examples of characters who left their respective shows early. Name the characters who replaced them, and if you're so inclined, the actors who played them. Note: Some characters may have been replaced TWICE.

1. "Coach" Ernie Pantusso on *Cheers*
2. Diane Chambers on *Cheers*
3. "Trapper John" McIntire on *M*A*S*H*
4. Lieutenant Colonel Henry Blake on *M*A*S*H*
5. Major Frank Burns on *M*A*S*H*
6. Crissy Snow on *Three's Company*
7. The Ropers on *Three's Company*
8. Barney Fife on *The Andy Griffith Show*
9. Jill Munroe on *Charlie's Angels*
10. Sabrina Duncan on *Charlie's Angels*

11. Flo Castleberry on *Alice*
12. Charlie Moore on *Head of the Class*
13. Vinnie Barbarino on *Welcome Back Kotter*
14. Bo and Luke Duke on *The Dukes of Hazzard*
15. Mrs. Edna Garrett on *The Facts of Life*
16. Court officer Selma Hacker on *Night Court*
17. Public defender Liz Williams on *Night Court*
18. Valerie Hogan on *Valerie*
19. Chico Rodriguez on *Chico and the Man*
20. Dr. Joel Fleischmann on *Northern Exposure*

MILITARY MUSTER

On your feet, soldier! Identify the fifteen military-themed TV shows described below, and that's an order!

1. Hospital hijinks in war-torn Korea
2. Dimwitted Mayberry transplant became a Marine
3. World War II POWs outfoxed some wacky Nazis.
4. Ernest Borgnine, Gavin McLeod, and Tim Conway were stationed in the South Pacific.
5. A con-artist sergeant devised schemes at Fort Baxter.
6. Gerald McRaney sitcom that incorporated the Gulf War into some of its plots
7. Don Rickles played a Navy drill instructor, you hockey puck!
8. The trials and tribulations of the women in Vietnam
9. Larry Storch and Ken Berry were silly cavalrymen.
10. Sitcom based on a Goldie Hawn movie
11. Vic Morrow played Sgt. Chip Saunders.
12. This short-lived series, co-starring Jamie Lee Curtis, was set on a pink submarine.
13. Christopher George fought in the desert.
14. WWII pilot Robert Conrad headed a group of military troublemakers.
15. Navy lawyers dispensed justice in this '90s acronym-named series.

ANSWERS

1. *M*A*S*H*
2. Gomer Pyle, USMC
3. Hogan's Heroes
4. McHale's Navy
5. The Phil Silvers Show or
6. Major Dad
7. CPO Sharkey
8. China Beach
9. F Troop
10. Private Benjamin
11. Combat
12. Operation: Petticoat
13. The Rat Patrol
14. Baa Baa Black Sheep or Black Sheep Squadron
15. JAG

Another Incredible TV Spiral of Fun

Starting with #1, name a TV show in which both Michael J. Fox and Justine Bateman were featured regularly. Continue this pattern for Justine Bateman and Ron Eldard, and the rest of the spiral, until you reach Pam Dawber. Then reward yourself with a snack.

Jimmy Smits

Michael J. Fox

1. _____

Justine Bateman

2. _____

Ron Eldard

3. _____

George Clooney

4. _____

Swoosie Kurtz

5. _____

Tony Randall

6. _____

Diana Muldaur

7. _____

Dennis Weaver

8. _____

Burt Reynolds

9. _____

Marilu Henner

10. _____

Judd Hirsch

11. _____

Jere Burns

12. _____

Mel Harris

13. _____

Ken Olin

14. _____

Dennis Franz

15. _____

16. _____

Susan Dey

17. _____

Jay Thomas

18. _____

Pam Dawber

RANDOM TV FACTS, PART 4

Answer all these delightful TV trivia questions.

1. Who shot J. R. Ewing?
2. Who killed Laura Palmer?
3. How was Granny related to Jed Clampett, and what was her full name?
4. Where did Tony Nelson find Jeannie?
5. Who was Dr. Richard Kimble pursuing?
6. Who was married with kids, Cagney or Lacey?
7. Where was the Fonz's "office"?
8. How did you do the "Witches' Honor" sign on *Bewitched*?
9. Who didn't get fired from WJM in the last episode of *The Mary Tyler Moore Show*?
10. Name the Hackett brothers' and Roy Biggins's airlines on *Wings*.
11. How did Gary die on *thirtysomething*?
12. Who played Blossom's estranged mother?
13. What was Wonder Woman's alias?
14. What were Ralph's powers on *The Greatest American Hero*?
15. Name Niles Crane's oft-mentioned, but never-seen wife.
16. Before they moved to Beverly Hills, where did Brandon and Brenda Walsh live?
17. What high school did Zack, A. C., Screech, and Kelly attend?
18. Who narrated every episode of *The Wonder Years*?
19. Who is Bart Simpson's favorite superhero?
20. What's the name of Martin Payne's TV show?

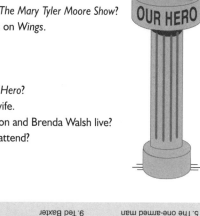

OUR HERO

ANSWERS

1. Kristen Shepherd (played by Mary Crosby)
2. Leland Palmer, her father
3. She was his mother-in-law. Her name was Daisy Moses.
4. In an ornate bottle on the beach
5. The one-armed man
6. Lacey
7. In the men's room at Arnold's
8. Make a "peace sign" with your left hand, then rest your hand on your face so that your fingers are on either side of your nose.
9. Ted Baxter
10. Hackett bros.—Sandpiper Air; Biggins—Aeromass
11. He was hit by a car while on his way to visit Nancy in the hospital.
12. Melissa Manchester
13. Diana Prince
14. Flight, X-ray vision, invisibility
15. Maris
16. Minneapolis, Minnesota
17. Bayside High School
18. Daniel Stern
19. Radioactive Man
20. *Speak Out*

MAXIMUM MINISERIES

Described below are fifteen hit TV miniseries. Identify them all.

1. Alex Haley traced his family history.
2. The first miniseries in which Robert Mitchum played a WWII naval officer
3. Sequel to #2
4. Richard Chamberlain hung out in Japan in the seventeenth century.
5. Jewish Peter Strauss and Roman Peter O'Toole did battle in 72 A.D.
6. Priest Richard Chamberlain fell for Rachel Ward.
7. Miniseries that posed the question: "What if Russia took over the U.S.?"
8. John Jakes's pre-Civil War novel turned into a miniseries starring Patrick Swayze.
9. Robert Duvall and Tommy Lee Jones drove cattle.
10. The sequel to *Gone with The Wind*
11. James Woods and Meryl Streep faced Nazi persecution.
12. A virus killed everyone except Gary Sinise, Molly Ringwald, and a guy who kept re-spelling the word *moon*.
13. The Visitors came from outer space to take over Earth.
14. James Garner was a U.S. Senator and Harry Hamlin was an astronaut in this James Michener-penned miniseries.
15. Angie Dickenson and Candice Bergen were the title characters of this Jackie Collins-novel based miniseries.

ANSWERS

1. *Roots*
2. *The Winds of War*
3. *War and Remembrance*
4. *Shogun*
5. *Masada*
6. *The Thorn Birds*
7. *Amerika*
8. *North and South*
9. *Lonesome Dove*
10. *Scarlett*
11. *Holocaust*
12. *The Stand*
13. *V*
14. *Space*
15. *The Hollywood Wives*

Yet More Random TV Facts

Answer these fun TV trivia questions.

1. Which Friend let it slip that Ross loved Rachel?

2. Whom did Benson hire as his aide when he became lieutenant governor?

3. What was unusual about the show *Roc* during the 1992–93 season?

4. What did Al Bundy do for a living?

5. Where did Paul and Jamie Buchman first meet?

6. What were the call letters of the radio station in *NewsRadio*?

7. What country was Balki from?

8. What was Ned and Stacey's agreement?

9. Which of Tim Taylor's boys went through a brief cancer scare?

10. Name the college and professional football teams coached by Hayden Fox.

11. In *The Golden Palace*, which of the original Golden Girls did not appear?

12. What did Jerry, Elaine, George, and Kramer refrain from in "The Contest," and who eventually won?

13. Name the college attended by Denise Huxtable on *A Different World*. How long did she attend?

14. What was the original name for Ellen DeGeneres's sitcom before it became *Ellen*?

15. What heroic act did Dr. Doug Ross perform that received major media attention?

ANSWERS

1. Chandler

2. Kraus, the housekeeper

3. It was broadcast live.

4. He sold shoes.

5. Two possible answers. As adults, they first met at a newstand in New York City. However, it was suggested in one episode that they briefly met as children in The Museum of Natural History. How romantic!

6. WNYX

7. Mypos

8. Ned would allow Stacey to live in his apartment if she

9. Randy

10. College team—Minnesota Screaming Eagles; Pro team—Orlando Breakers

11. Dorothy (played by Bea Arthur)

12. They refrained from—ahem!—masturbating. George won the contest.

13. Hillman College. She only went for a year.

14. *These Friends of Mine*

15. He saved a kid from drowning in a sewer.

Test Your
Movie IQ!

RHYMIN' DOUBLE FEATURES

Here's a unique film festival idea that's actually pretty stupid. The title of each movie described in the left column rhymes with the title of a movie described in the right column. Match the rhyming pairs, then rent <u>Going Ape!</u> and <u>What's Eating Gilbert Grape?</u>

NOW SHOWING
ERASERHEAD
and
DROP DEAD FRED

1. Cher won an Oscar for this
2. Australian horse movie with Kirk Douglas
3. Movie extension of *Police Squad!*
4. Gene Kelly/Debbie Reynolds musical
5. Half-man, half-machine Detroit cop
6. Classic Gary Cooper western
7. Yuletide tale about a boy who wants a BB gun
8. Danny and Sandy fell in love in the 1950s
9. Charles Bronson vigilante flick
10. Danny DeVito-directed divorce yarn
11. Undersea epic by James Cameron
12. Ernest Borgnine won an Oscar for this
13. Michael Douglas was on a rampage in L.A.
14. Horror movie about sideshow attractions
15. Dennis Quaid/Lou Gossett, Jr. sci-fi film

A. Brooke Shields was stranded on an island
B. Kid 'N' Play vehicle
C. Dolph Lundgren fought a hostile alien
D. Ryan O'Neal designed see-thru jeans
E. John Candy babysat for his brother's kids
F. Denzel Washington fought in the Civil War
G. Mickey Rourke/Kim Basinger film
H. Sharon Stone played a voyeur
I. Hitchcock film with a runaway carousel
J. Jack Nicholson/Roman Polanski film
K. Dudley Moore played a biblical figure
L. Stallone competed in arm-wrestling
M. Sean Connery/Wesley Snipes film
N. 1993 John Sayles film
O. Meg Ryan/Alec Baldwin film

ANSWERS

THE INCREDIBLE MOVIE CHAIN #1

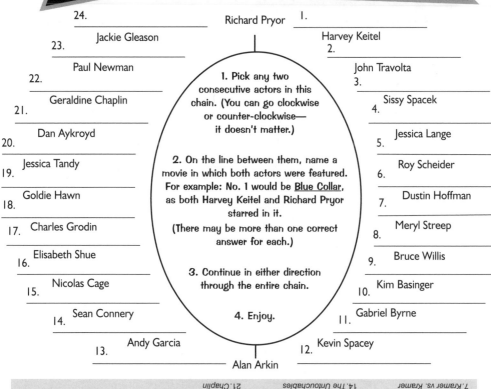

24. _____ Richard Pryor 1. _____

23. Jackie Gleason   Harvey Keitel
                                        2. _____

22. Paul Newman   John Travolta
                                        3. _____

21. Geraldine Chaplin   Sissy Spacek
                                        4. _____

20. Dan Aykroyd   Jessica Lange
                                        5. _____

19. Jessica Tandy   Roy Scheider
                                        6. _____

18. Goldie Hawn   Dustin Hoffman
                                        7. _____

17. Charles Grodin   Meryl Streep
                                        8. _____

16. Elisabeth Shue   Bruce Willis
                                        9. _____

15. Nicolas Cage   Kim Basinger
                                        10. _____

14. Sean Connery   Gabriel Byrne
                                        11. _____

13. Andy Garcia   Kevin Spacey
                                        12. _____

Alan Arkin

1. Pick any two consecutive actors in this chain. (You can go clockwise or counter-clockwise—it doesn't matter.)

2. On the line between them, name a movie in which both actors were featured. For example: No. 1 would be <u>Blue Collar</u>, as both Harvey Keitel and Richard Pryor starred in it.

(There may be more than one correct answer for each.)

3. Continue in either direction through the entire chain.

4. Enjoy.

Bad Movie Bonanza

Hey, they can't all be gems. Match the actors with the bad movies (listed below) in which they appeared.

____ 1. Dustin Hoffman
____ 2. Billy Crystal
____ 3. Shirley MacLaine
____ 4. Kevin Costner
____ 5. Faye Dunaway
____ 6. Meryl Streep
____ 7. Meg Ryan
____ 8. Arnold Schwarzenegger
____ 9. Denzel Washington
____ 10. Michael Caine
____ 11. Susan Sarandon
____ 12. Robert De Niro
____ 13. Jack Nicholson

____ 14. Michelle Pfeiffer
____ 15. Tom Hanks
____ 16. Sean Connery
____ 17. Danny DeVito
____ 18. Anjelica Huston
____ 19. Anthony Hopkins
____ 20. Clint Eastwood
____ 21. Al Pacino
____ 22. Tom Cruise
____ 23. Donald Sutherland
____ 24. Gene Hackman
____ 25. Marlon Brando

A. *The Hollywood Knights*
B. *Going Ape!*
C. *She-Devil*
D. *He Knows You're Alone*
E. *Francis In the Navy*
F. *Meteor*
G. *Christopher Columbus: The Discovery*
H. *Amityville 3-D*

I. *Doctors' Wives*
J. *Sizzle Beach U.S.A.*
K. *Supergirl*
L. *Bloody Mama*
M. *Cannonball Run II*
N. *The Ice Pirates*
O. *Cruising*
P. *Audrey Rose*
Q. *The Hand*

R. *Dr. Terror's House of Horrors*
S. *Hell's Angels on Wheels*
T. *Carbon Copy*
U. *Ishtar*
V. *The Other Side of Midnight*
W. *Losin' It*
X. *Rabbit Test*
Y. *Hercules in New York*

BY THE NUMBERS

Fill in the correct numbers to complete the movie titles below. When you've finished, add together all the numbers in Column A. Do the same for Column B. Subtract the total from Column B from the total from Column A to get the name of another numerical movie.

Column A

1. *Passenger ___*
2. *___ Flew over the Cuckoo's Nest*
3. *Deep Star ___*
4. *The ___ Blows*
5. *The Beast from ___ Fathoms*
6. *___ Men and a Baby*
7. *___ Years, B.C.*
8. *The ___ Samurai*
9. *Catch-___*
10. *Plan ___ from Outer Space*
11. *___ Seconds over Tokyo*
12. *The ___ Chairs (Mel Brooks version)*
13. *Stalag ___*
14. *The ___ Jakes*
15. *___ Maniacs*
16. *___ Candles*
17. *___ Again!*
18. *___ Men Out*
19. *Less Than ___*

THE EQUATION

Column A Total

minus

Column B Total

equals

Mystery

Numerical Movie Title

_____

Column B

1. *___ Dalmations*
2. *___ Motels*
3. *The ___ Steps*
4. *___ : A Space Odyssey*
5. *___ Easy Pieces*
6. *___ Weeks (Dudley Moore vehicle)*
7. *___ Rooms*
8. *The Man with ___ Brains*
9. *The ___ Faces of Dr. Lao*
10. *___ HRS.*
11. *Bat ___*
12. *The $ ___ Duck*
13. *___ Charlie Mopic*
14. *___ Coins in a Fountain*
15. *The ___ Seasons*
16. *___ Corners*
17. *___ Leagues under the Sea*
18. *The ___ Commandments*
19. *___ Pick-Up*
20. *With ___ You Get Eggroll*

THE ROLE-PLAYING GAME

The following are twenty groups of famous film roles. In each group, only one actor has played all three roles. Name the actor, and the respective movies.

1. A cartoon caveman, an exterminator, and the King of England

2. A subway token vendor, a computer expert, and a brilliant law student

3. A TV news anchor, a Florida lawyer, and a gay window dresser

4. A Navy pilot, a bartender, and an Irish immigrant

5. A stuntman, a sheriff, and a stockcar driver

6. An English teacher, a boy trapped in a board game, and a sailorman

7. An Olympic coach, a polka bandleader, and a shower-curtain-ring salesman

8. An FBI trainee, a carny, and a 12-year-old prostitute

9. A pool shark, a hockey star, and a prisoner

10. A school principal, a Civil War soldier, and a chauffeur

11. A pianist, a hit man, and a book-editing werewolf

12. A country music singer, a soccer-playing P.O.W., and a mountain climber

13. A dog trainer, a science reporter, and a ghost

14. A brain surgeon, a TV weatherman, and a fire chief

15. A secretary, a court-appointed psychiatrist, and a forty-first century space adventurer

16. A stripper, a sexually harassing boss, and Hester Prynne

17. An artist with cerebral palsy, an honorary Mohican, and a farmer

18. A cloned construction worker, a man dying of cancer, and a psychotic tenant

19. A Nazi commandant, a game show contestant, and a dealer in virtual reality

20. A soap opera star, a textile worker, and a cotton farmer

ANSWERS

1. **John Goodman** (The Flintstones, Arachnophobia, King Ralph)
2. **Sandra Bullock** (While You Were Sleeping, The Net, A Time to Kill)
3. **William Hurt** (Broadcast News, Body Heat, Kiss of the Spider Woman)
4. **Tom Cruise** (Top Gun, Cocktail, Far and Away)
5. **Burt Reynolds** (Hooper, The Best Little Whorehouse in Texas, Stroker Ace)
6. **Robin Williams** (Dead Poets Society, Jumanji, Popeye)
7. **John Candy** (Cool Runnings; Home Alone: Planes, Trains, and Automobiles)
8. **Jodie Foster** (Silence of the Lambs, Carny, Taxi Driver)
9. **Paul Newman** (The Hustler, Slap Shot, Cool Hand Luke)
10. **Morgan Freeman** (Lean on Me, Glory, Driving Miss Daisy)
11. **Sylvester Stallone** (Rhinestone, Victory, Cliffhanger)
12. **Jack Nicholson** (Five Easy Pieces, Prizzi's Honor, Wolf)
13. **Geena Davis** (The Accidental Tourist, The Fly, Beetlejuice)
14. **Steve Martin** (The Man with Two Brains, L.A. Story, Roxanne)
15. **Jane Fonda** (9 to 5, Agnes of God, Barbarella)
16. **Demi Moore** (Striptease, Disclosure, The Scarlet Letter)
17. **Daniel-Day Lewis** (My Left Foot, The Last of the Mohicans, The Crucible)
18. **Michael Keaton** (Multiplicity, My Life, Pacific Heights)
19. **Ralph Fiennes** (Schindler's List, Quiz Show, Strange Days)
20. **Sally Field** (Soapdish, Norma Rae, Places in the Heart)

The Incredible Movie Chain Strikes Back

24. _____

Henry Winkler   1. _____

23.   Sylvester Stallone

Shelley Long
2. _____

22.   Sharon Stone

Tom Hanks
3. _____

21.   Michael Douglas

4.   Corey Feldman

20.   Glenn Close

5.   Jason Robards

19.   Robert Redford

6.   Steve Martin

18.   Michelle Pfeiffer

7.   Christopher Walken

17.   Mel Gibson

8.   Martin Sheen

16.   Sigourney Weaver

9.   Drew Barrymore

15.   Harrison Ford

10.   Ryan O'Neal

14.   Sean Young

11.   Bruce Dern

13.   Bill Murray

12.   Robert Shaw

Richard Dreyfuss

1. Pick any two consecutive actors in this chain. (You can go clockwise or counter-clockwise— it doesn't matter.)

2. On the line between them, name a movie in which both actors were featured. For example: No. 1 would be <u>Night Shift</u>, as both Henry Winkler and Shelley Long starred in it.
(There may be more than one correct answer for each.)

3. Continue in either direction through the entire chain.

4. Enjoy.

ANSWERS

1. Night Shift
2. The Money Pit
3. The 'burbs
4. Dream a Little Dream
5. Parenthood
6. Pennies from Heaven
7. The Dead Zone
8. Firestarter
9. Irreconcilable Differences
10. The Driver
11. Black Sunday
12. Jaws
13. What About Bob?
14. Stripes
15. Blade Runner
16. Working Girl
17. The Year of Living Dangerously
18. Tequila Sunrise
19. Up Close and Personal
20. The Natural
21. Fatal Attraction
22. Basic Instinct
23. The Specialist
24. The Lords of Flatbush

OH, THOSE ANGST-RIDDEN MOVIE TEENS!

Described below are teen-angst movies. Identify them all.

1. A brain, a jock, a popular girl, a delinquent, and an outcast talk things out during Saturday detention.
2. A girl turns sixteen, but no one remembers.
3. A shy boy gets out his aggression on his pirate radio station.
4. A suburban lad turns his house into a brothel while his parents are away.
5. A popular boy plays hookey from school and tools around Chicago.
6. A popular girl and the new kid in town cause a rash of high school "suicides."
7. A punker boy from Hollywood falls for a girl from the L.A. suburbs.
8. An unusual girl is courted by the richest boy in town and a boy named Ducky.
9. Eric Stoltz falls for Lea Thompson while Mary Stuart Masterson pines for him.
10. An aimless boy who kickboxes falls for the smartest girl in school.
11. A stoner disrupts class by ordering a pizza.
12. A teen kills his girlfriend, but his stoned buddies don't notify the authorities.
13. Leonardo DiCaprio re-enacts Jim Carroll's days of youth.
14. Angst-ridden prep school boys embrace literature at the prompting of their English teacher.
15. Indiana high-school graduates compete against college boys in a bicycle race.
16. Martin Hewitt becomes obsessed with Brooke Shields.
17. A prep-school boy has an affair with his roommate's mother.
18. A Scottish boy falls for the best player on his soccer team—a girl!
19. Lori Loughlin writes friend C. Thomas Howell a confession of love, but he thinks it was written by Kelly Preston.
20. Four teenage girls use witchcraft to get revenge on their classmates.

ANSWERS

1. The Breakfast Club
2. Sixteen Candles
3. Pump Up the Volume
4. Risky Business
5. Ferris Bueller's Day Off
6. Heathers
7. Valley Girl
8. Pretty in Pink
9. Some Kind of Wonderful
10. Say Anything
11. Fast Times at Ridgemont High
12. River's Edge
13. The Basketball Diaries
14. Dead Poets Society
15. Breaking Away
16. Endless Love
17. Class
18. Gregory's Girl
19. Secret Admirer
20. The Craft

MOVIE SEQUELS 2: AFTER THE COLON

Whenever those clever movie executives want to spruce up the title of a movie sequel, they add a colon and a subtitle after the main title (Example: Die Hard 2: Die Harder). We've provided the subtitles, you provide the first part. Remember to get the sequel number correct or you don't get full credit.

1. _____	: Season of the Witch
2. _____	: Assignment: Miami Beach
3. _____	: Judgment Day
4. _____	: Jason Takes Manhattan
5. _____	: The Quest for Peace
6. _____	: On the Rocks
7. _____	: Lost in New York
8. _____	: The Dream Warriors
9. _____	: The Final Insult
10. _____	: The Voyage Home
11. _____	: The Quickening
12. _____	: Dark Territory
13. _____	: The Possession
14. _____	: The Heretic
15. _____	: Better Watch Out!
16. _____	: On the Move
17. _____	: Dead by Dawn
18. _____	: Toulon's Revenge
19. _____	: The New Batch
20. _____	: The Next Day

N '93

ANSWERS

1. Halloween 3
2. Police Academy 5
3. Terminator 2
4. Friday the 13th, Part 8
5. Superman 4

6. Arthur 2
7. Home Alone 2
8. A Nightmare on Elm Street 3
9. Naked Gun 33 1/3
10. Star Trek 4

11. Highlander 2
12. Under Siege 2
13. Amityville 2
14. Exorcist 2
15. Silent Night, Deadly Night 3

16. Mannequin 2
17. Evil Dead 2
18. Puppet Master III
19. Gremlins 2
20. Porky's 2

Alien Life Forms

Name the movies in which creatures from outer space perform these acts:

1. Make bicycles fly
2. Incubate young in human's chest
3. Use five musical notes to communicate with earthlings
4. Turn people into emotionless pod people
5. Proclaim *Klaatu Barada Nikto*
6. Bring new life to old folks with pupal stage
7. Bring a dead deer back to life
8. Do Jimmy Durante impressions
9. Terrorize Antarctic research team
10. Use camouflage to hunt Arnold Schwarzenegger
11. Form cop team with human officer
12. Remain dead in trunk of car
13. Ooze and expand to cover an entire town
14. Help residents of New York tenement save their home
15. Blow up L.A., N.Y.C., and D.C.
16. Derive chemical energy from human orgasms
17. Come to Earth to obtain water for dying planet; become addicted to TV and alcohol instead
18. Pose as FBI agent to track down vicious alien who invades human hosts
19. Observe race relations in Harlem
20. Resurrect dead people to conquer Earth; fly paper-plate-shaped saucers

THE INCREDIBLE MOVIE CHAIN RETURNS!

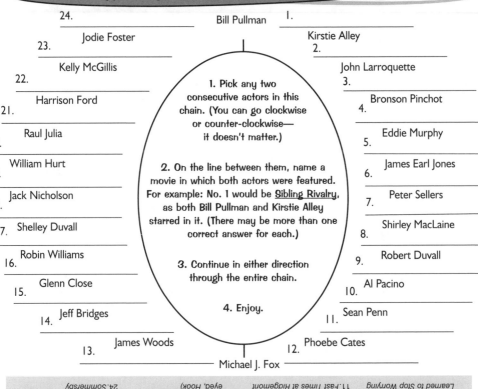

24. _____ Jodie Foster
23. _____ Kelly McGillis
22. _____ Harrison Ford
21. _____ Raul Julia
20. _____ William Hurt
19. _____ Jack Nicholson
18. _____ Shelley Duvall
17. _____ Robin Williams
16. _____ Glenn Close
15. _____ Jeff Bridges
14. _____ James Woods
13. _____

Bill Pullman

Kirstie Alley
John Larroquette
Bronson Pinchot
Eddie Murphy
James Earl Jones
Peter Sellers
Shirley MacLaine
Robert Duvall
Al Pacino
Sean Penn
Phoebe Cates

Michael J. Fox

1. Pick any two consecutive actors in this chain. (You can go clockwise or counter-clockwise—it doesn't matter.)

2. On the line between them, name a movie in which both actors were featured. For example: No. 1 would be <u>Sibling Rivalry</u>, as both Bill Pullman and Kirstie Alley starred in it. (There may be more than one correct answer for each.)

3. Continue in either direction through the entire chain.

4. Enjoy.

A MAN CALLED SPIELBERG

Part 1: Name the Steven Spielberg-directed movie that features the following images:

1. A ferris wheel rolling out of control
2. A mashed-potato replica of Devil's Tower
3. A cave full of large insects
4. A one-eyed corpse floating in a sunken boat
5. Seagulls impeding an enemy plane
6. A young boy hiding from Nazis in a pool of human waste
7. Red car struggling to get up hill while being chased by a semi-truck
8. A multi-colored food fight
9. *Tyrannosaurus rex* devouring a lawyer
10. Melting Nazis

Part 2: Name the Spielberg-produced movie that features:

1. A car vs. skateboard chase through a '50s town square
2. Scary spiders that eat cats
3. A youthful Baker Street sleuth
4. A cool underground pirate ship
5. A bathtub falling through the floor of a crumbling house
6. Bigfoot in a domestic setting
7. A creepy clown doll under the bed
8. An evil creature exploded in a microwave

ANSWERS

Part 1
1. *1941*
2. *Close Encounters of the Third Kind*
3. *Indiana Jones and the Temple of Doom*
4. *Jaws*
5. *Indiana Jones and the Last Crusade*
6. *Schindler's List*
7. *Duel*
8. *Hook*
9. *Jurassic Park*
10. *Raiders of the Lost Ark*

Part 2
1. *Back to the Future*
2. *Arachnophobia*
3. *Young Sherlock Holmes*
4. *The Goonies*
5. *The Money Pit*
6. *Harry and the Hendersons*
7. *Poltergeist*
8. *Gremlins*

"The" Quiz

Each of the movies described below is titled "The _____," with a single word needed to fill the blank. Complete the titles for the movies described. When you're done, the first letters of each word you've supplied, when read in order, will provide a cryptic clue to one more movie title beginning with "The."

1. Modern Irish youths form a '60s-style rhythm and blues group   The _____
2. Jack Lemmon lends his abode to philandering coworkers   The _____
3. Robert Redford destroys baseball park lighting system   The _____
4. Cyborg from future hunts Sarah Conner   The _____
5. Clint Eastwood/Charlie Sheen buddy flick   The _____
6. Linda Blair's head rotates   The _____
7. John Carpenter film about ghostly shipwreck   The _____
8. Elliot Ness goes after Capone   The _____
9. Jack Nicholson wields an ax   The _____
10. Burt Reynolds tries to kill himself   The _____
11. Sting plays Dr. Frankenstein   The _____
12. Disney mice save kidnapped girl   The _____
13. Christopher Reeve is a pilot in 1928   The _____
14. Macauley Culkin does ballet   The _____
15. Oliver Stone's homage to dead rock star   The _____
16. Gregory Peck fathers the anti-Christ   The _____
17. Disaster flick about killer bee invasion   The _____
18. Howard Hughes western featuring Jane Russell's cleavage   The _____
19. Tom Cruise exposes Mafia lawyers   The _____
20. Jeff Goldblum metamorphoses into insect   The _____
21. Third Dirty Harry movie   The _____
22. 1991 adventure with jet-pack wearing hero   The _____
BONUS CLUE: Can't refuse Brando's offer   The _____

ANSWERS

1. The Commitments
2. The Apartment
3. The Natural
4. The Terminator
5. The Rookie
6. The Exorcist
7. The Fog
8. The Untouchables
9. The Shining
10. The End
11. The Bride
12. The Rescuers
13. The Aviator
14. The Nutcracker
15. The Doors
16. The Omen
17. The Swarm
18. The Outlaw
19. The Firm
20. The Fly
21. The Enforcer
22. The Rocketeer
BONUS ANSWER: The Godfather

TOURIST ATTRACTIONS

Following are descriptions of U.S. landmarks and tourist attractions. Use these clues to name all fifteen attractions, then load a cooler with soda pop and take a road trip.

1. Where aliens landed in *Close Encounters of the Third Kind*
2. 007 protected this in *Goldfinger.*
3. Its remains provided ironic twist in *Planet of the Apes.*
4. King Kong fell from this in 1976.
5. Pee Wee Herman wanted to see its basement in his big adventure.
6. Site of final showdown in *The Warriors*
7. Lex Luthor dropped a bomb on this in *Superman.*
8. Cary Grant rescued Eva Marie Saint here in *North by Northwest.*
9. In a 1996 film, Ed Harris aimed chemical weapons at San Francisco from here.
10. Title and motif of Danny Glover/Kevin Kline film
11. Ferris and friends caught a game here on his day off
12. Meeting place in *An Affair to Remember*
13. Where Albert Brooks and Julie Hagerty fought in *Lost in America*
14. Spinal Tap sang "Heartbreak Hotel" here.
15. Tony Curtis evaded mobsters here in *Forty Pounds of Trouble.*

BAD SPORTS

Match the famous athlete with the feature film in which he or she appeared.

_____ 1. O. J. Simpson
_____ 2. Kareem Abdul-Jabbar
_____ 3. Lyle Alzado
_____ 4. Joe Namath
_____ 5. Bruce Jenner
_____ 6. Greg Louganis
_____ 7. Terry Bradshaw
_____ 8. Alex Karras
_____ 9. Fred Dryer
_____ 10. Ken Norton
_____ 11. Muhammed Ali
_____ 12. Rosie Grier
_____ 13. Mary Lou Retton
_____ 14. Brian Bosworth
_____ 15. Wilt Chamberlain
_____ 16. Julius Irving
_____ 17. Pelé
_____ 18. Ray Nitschke
_____ 19. Meadowlark Lemon
_____ 20. Joe DiMaggio

A. _Dirty Laundry_
B. _The Towering Inferno_
C. _Death Before Dishonor_
D. _Conan the Destroyer_
E. _Avalanche Express_
F. _Manhattan Merry-Go-Round_
G. _Hooper_
H. _Airplane_
I. _Stone Cold_
J. _Doin' Time_
K. _The Thing with Two Heads_
L. _Victory_
M. _Ernest Goes to Camp_
N. _Can't Stop the Music_
O. _Modern Romance_
P. _Philadelphia_
Q. _Mandingo_
R. _Hootch Country Boys_
S. _Scrooged_
T. _The Longest Yard_

GEEK MOVIES OF THE '80s

Match the computer/techno geek movie on the right with its description on the left.

1. Man buys computer; computer woos his pretty neighbor
2. Young man at trailer park gets high score on video game, then he's recruited to save the universe
3. Video-game creator is zapped into a computer
4. Horny teens hang out at the arcade
5. Teenage boy accesses National Defense computer; nearly starts WWIII
6. Boy gets courage from fatherly video game character to fight real crooks
7. Half boy/half robot assimilates into the real world
8. Teen geeks use a computer to make a woman
9. Brilliant college students thwart plans to use lasers as weapons
10. Two dumb teens time-travel in a phone booth
11. Defense robot gets struck by lightning; becomes sentient being
12. Geeks undo jock frat with techno advances
13. Teens must survive accidental space shuttle launch
14. Three boys build spaceship to visit outer space
15. Boy and his autistic brother go on a cross-country odyssey to a video game tournament

A. *Tron*
B. *D.A.R.Y.L.*
C. *The Wizard*
D. *Electric Dreams*
E. *Space Camp*
F. *Joysticks*
G. *Explorers*
H. *Bill & Ted's Excellent Adventure*
I. *Revenge of the Nerds*
J. *War Games*
K. *Weird Science*
L. *Short Circuit*
M. *Real Genius*
N. *Cloak & Dagger*
O. *The Last Starfighter*

BOY-GIRL-BOY-GIRL

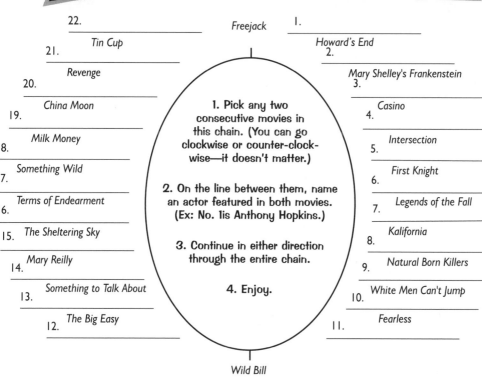

22. _____
   Tin Cup
21. _____
   Revenge
20. _____
   China Moon
19. _____
   Milk Money
18. _____
   Something Wild
17. _____
   Terms of Endearment
16. _____
   The Sheltering Sky
15. _____
   Mary Reilly
14. _____
   Something to Talk About
13. _____
   The Big Easy
12. _____

Freejack

1. _____
   Howard's End
2. _____
   Mary Shelley's Frankenstein
3. _____
   Casino
4. _____
   Intersection
5. _____
   First Knight
6. _____
   Legends of the Fall
7. _____
   Kalifornia
8. _____
   Natural Born Killers
9. _____
   White Men Can't Jump
10. _____
   Fearless
11. _____

1. Pick any two consecutive movies in this chain. (You can go clockwise or counter-clockwise—it doesn't matter.)

2. On the line between them, name an actor featured in both movies. (Ex: No. 1 is Anthony Hopkins.)

3. Continue in either direction through the entire chain.

4. Enjoy.

Wild Bill

A Director's Stable

Each of the groups of actors listed below is closely associated with the films of a certain director. Identify all twenty directors from their "stables" of favorite actors, then study <u>auteur</u> theory in film class.

1. Robert De Niro, Harvey Keitel, Joe Pesci

2. Kyle MacLachlan, Laura Dern, Jack Nance

3. Divine, Mink Stole, Ricki Lake

4. Molly Ringwald, Anthony Michael Hall, John Candy

5. Peter Sellers, Julie Andrews, Dudley Moore

6. Diane Keaton, Mia Farrow, Louise Lasser

7. Marty Feldman, Dom DeLuise, Gene Wilder, Harvey Korman

8. Wesley Snipes, Ruby Dee, Ossie Davis, Delroy Lindo, John Turturro

9. John Lurie, Roberto Benigni, Tom Waits

10. Arnold Schwarzenegger, Bill Paxton, Michael Biehn, Linda Hamilton

11. Adrienne Barbeau, Kurt Russell, Jamie Lee Curtis

12. Tor Johnson, Bela Lugosi, Criswell

13. Agnes Moorhead, Joseph Cotten, Ray Collins

14. James Stewart, Gary Cooper, Lionel Barrymore, Jean Arthur

15. Rock Hudson, Jane Wyman, Barbara Rush

16. John Wayne, Ward Bond, Henry Fonda

17. Grace Kelly, Tippi Hedren, James Stewart, Cary Grant

18. Elliot Gould, Shelley Duvall, Tim Robbins

19. Cybill Shepherd, Ryan O'Neal, John Ritter

20. Gena Rowlands, Peter Falk, Ben Gazzara

ANSWERS

1. Martin Scorsese
2. David Lynch
3. John Waters
4. John Hughes
5. Blake Edwards
6. Woody Allen
7. Mel Brooks
8. Spike Lee
9. Jim Jarmusch
10. James Cameron
11. John Carpenter
12. Ed Wood, Jr.
13. Orson Welles
14. Frank Capra
15. Douglas Sirk
16. John Ford
17. Alfred Hitchcock
18. Robert Altman
19. Peter Bogdanovich
20. John Cassavetes

CHOOSE YOUR WEAPON

In each of the movies listed in the left column, a character uses one of the unusual weapons listed in the right column. Match them up.

1. *A Clockwork Orange*
2. *The Wizard of Oz*
3. *Heathers*
4. *2001: A Space Odyssey*
5. *Goldfinger*
6. *Single White Female*
7. *Die Hard 2: Die Harder*
8. *Wild at Heart*
9. *Body Double*
10. *Basic Instinct*
11. *Basket Case*
12. *Monty Python and the Holy Grail*
13. *Misery*
14. *Crocodile Dundee*
15. *Indiana Jones and the Last Crusade*
16. *Dial "M" for Murder*
17. *Batman*
18. *One Flew Over the Cuckoo's Nest*
19. *The Road Warrior*
20. *Black Sunday*

A. Razor-sharp hat
B. Typewriter
C. Boomerang
D. Scissors
E. Acidic cosmetics
F. Blimp
G. Pillow
H. Umbrella
I. Mug of detergent
J. High-heeled shoe
K. Bucket of water
L. Phallic sculpture
M. Bone
N. Concrete floor
O. Industrial power drill
P. Scalpel
Q. Icicle
R. Canned food item
S. Ice pick
T. Cow

ANSWERS

20. F	15. H	10. S	5. A
19. C	14. R	9. O	4. M
18. G	13. B	8. N	3. I
17. E	12. T	7. Q	2. K
16. D	11. P	6. J	1. L

ONE WORD LEADS TO ANOTHER

Described below are twenty movies with one-word titles. Each title begins with a different letter of the alphabet. After you've identified all twenty movies, the six remaining unused letters, when unscrambled, will spell another one-word movie title.

_____ 1. Marshal Sean Connery fights bad guys on Jupiter's moon.

_____ 2. 1992 Clint Eastwood western

_____ 3. Kevin Bacon plays a hotshot bicycle messenger.

_____ 4. On its poster, a girl wearing heart-shaped glasses sucks a lollipop.

_____ 5. Hitchcock film in which Jimmy Stewart is afraid of heights

_____ 6. Contains "The Sorcerer's Apprentice"

_____ 7. Olivia Newton-John persuades Gene Kelly to open a roller disco.

_____ 8. Humphrey Bogart–Ingrid Bergman classic

_____ 9. This rat movie had a sequel called *Ben*.

_____ 10. Scott Baio uses telekinesis to undress women.

_____ 11. "Dueling Banjos" is its signature tune.

_____ 12. Rob Lowe leaves the farm to play hockey.

_____ 13. Don't get 'em wet, feed 'em after midnight, or expose 'em to bright light.

_____ 14. Peter Finch kills himself on live television.

_____ 15. 1982 horror film that popularized the phrase, "They're *here*."

_____ 16. Arnold Schwarzenegger plays a witness protection agent.

_____ 17. David Caruso movie written by Joe Eszterhas

_____ 18. Robert Redford is a golden-haired prison warden.

_____ 19. Woody Allen dates Mariel Hemingway.

_____ 20. Jane Fonda plays a cool-headed prostitute.

Remaining letters: ___ ___ ___ ___ ___ ___

Revenge of the Incredible Movie Chain

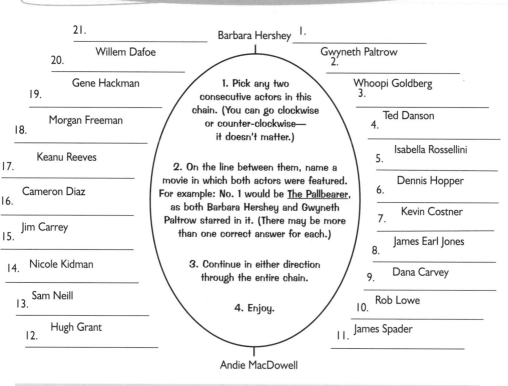

21. _____
Willem Dafoe
20. _____
Gene Hackman
19. _____
Morgan Freeman
18. _____
Keanu Reeves
17. _____
Cameron Diaz
16. _____
Jim Carrey
15. _____
Nicole Kidman
14.
Sam Neill
13.
Hugh Grant
12. _____

Andie MacDowell

Barbara Hershey 1.
_____
Gwyneth Paltrow
2. _____
Whoopi Goldberg
3. _____
Ted Danson
4. _____
Isabella Rossellini
5. _____
Dennis Hopper
6. _____
Kevin Costner
7. _____
James Earl Jones
8. _____
Dana Carvey
9. _____
Rob Lowe
10. _____
James Spader
11. _____

1. Pick any two consecutive actors in this chain. (You can go clockwise or counter-clockwise—it doesn't matter.)

2. On the line between them, name a movie in which both actors were featured. For example: No. 1 would be The Pallbearer, as both Barbara Hershey and Gwyneth Paltrow starred in it. (There may be more than one correct answer for each.)

3. Continue in either direction through the entire chain.

4. Enjoy.

ANSWERS

1. The Pallbearer
2. Moonlight and Valentino
3. Made in America
4. Cousins
5. Blue Velvet
6. Waterworld
7. Field of Dreams
8. Clean Slate
9. Wayne's World
10. Bad Influence
11. sex, lies, and videotape
12. Four Weddings and a Funeral
13. Sirens or Restoration
14. Dead Calm
15. Batman Forever
16. The Mask
17. Feeling Minnesota
18. Chain Reaction
19. Unforgiven
20. Mississippi Burning
21. The Last Temptation of Christ

SONG TITLE MOVIES

If you want audiences to remember your movie, name it after a popular song. The fifteen movies described below are examples of this phenomenon. Identify them all.

1. A prostitute poses as a rich businessman's girlfriend.

2. At a class reunion, a middle-aged woman is transported back in time to her high school days.

3. A narcoleptic gigolo travels with a millionaire's son.

4. The daughter of a mortician grows up in the 1970s.

5. Four preteen boys travel to see a dead body.

6. A computer programmer is contacted by a spy via her computer.

7. An alcoholic is "enabled" by her doting husband.

8. A nerdy geek pays a popular girl to be his girlfriend.

9. L.A. cop is frozen, then thawed in the future to defeat his arch nemesis.

10. A mobster informant hides in the suburbs under the Witness Protection Program.

11. An ex-con finds a yuppie's organizer and assumes his identity.

12. Workers at an Iowa brewery revolt against management.

13. A Chicago cop falls in love, despite the protests of his live-in mother.

14. A dead man reunites with his wife after he is reincarnated as her daughter's boyfriend.

15. A Caribbean police officer searches for his criminal boyhood friend.

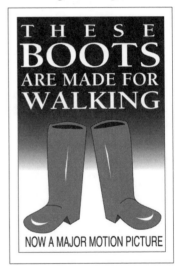

THESE
BOOTS
ARE MADE FOR
WALKING

NOW A MAJOR MOTION PICTURE

HISTORIC ROLES

Listed below are sixteen groups of historic figures. For each group, name the actor who portrayed all the historic figures in feature films, then name the respective films.

1. Al Capone, Jake LaMotta
2. Frances Farmer, Patsy Cline
3. Joan Crawford, Bonnie Parker
4. Malcolm X, Stephen Biko
5. Sid Vicious, Lee Harvey Oswald
6. Glenn Miller, Charles Lindbergh
7. Butch Cassidy, Earl K. Long
8. H. G. Wells, the Emperor Caligula
9. Lenny Bruce, Carl Bernstein
10. Moses, Michelangelo
11. Lon Chaney, George M. Cohan
12. Jimmy Hoffa, Eugene O'Neill
13. Jerry Lee Lewis, Gordon Cooper
14. Dian Fossey, Queen Isabella
15. Elvis Presley, Jim Morrison, Doc Holliday
16. Pablo Picasso, Richard Nixon, C. S. Lewis

ANSWERS

1. Robert De Niro (The Untouchables, Raging Bull)
2. Jessica Lange (Frances, Sweet Dreams)
3. Faye Dunaway (Mommie Dearest, Bonnie and Clyde)
4. Denzel Washington (Malcolm X, Cry Freedom)
5. Gary Oldman (Sid and Nancy, JFK)
6. James Stewart (The Glenn Miller Story, The Spirit of St. Louis)
7. Paul Newman (Butch Cassidy and the Sundance Kid, Blaze)
8. Malcolm McDowell (Time After Time, Caligula)
9. Dustin Hoffman (Lenny, All the President's Men)
10. Charlton Heston (The Ten Commandments, The Agony and the Ecstasy)
11. James Cagney (The Man of a Thousand Faces, Yankee Doodle Dandy)
12. Jack Nicholson (Hoffa, Reds)
13. Dennis Quaid (Great Balls of Fire, The Right Stuff)
14. Sigourney Weaver (Gorillas in the Mist, 1492: Conquest of Paradise)
15. Val Kilmer (True Romance, The Doors, Tombstone)
16. Anthony Hopkins (Surviving Picasso, Nixon, Shadowlands)

Co-Starring Countdown

How many movies did each of the following "star duos" perform in together? Enter that number in the space next to each duo.

HINT: Animated movies and voice-only performances should also be counted. For extra bonus fun, rattle off all the movies for each duo in a crowded place so you can impress strangers and passersby.

____ A. Meg Ryan and Dennis Quaid

____ B. Mia Farrow and Woody Allen

____ C. Dustin Hoffman and Al Pacino

____ D. Robert De Niro and Joe Pesci

____ E. Dom DeLuise and Burt Reynolds

____ F. Cheech and Chong

____ G. Michael Palin and John Cleese

____ H. Clint Eastwood and Sondra Locke

____ I. Samuel L. Jackson and Bruce Willis

____ J. Richard Pryor and Gene Wilder

ANSWERS

A. **3** (D.O.A.; Flesh and Bone; Innerspace)

B. **9** (Broadway Danny Rose; Crimes and Misdemeanors; Hannah and Her Sisters; Husbands and Wives; A Midsummer Night's Sex Comedy; New York Stories; Radio Days; Shadows and Fog; Zelig)

C. **1** (Dick Tracy)

D. **5** (A Bronx Tale; Casino; Goodfellas; Once Upon a Time in America; Raging Bull)

E. **7** (All Dogs Go to Heaven; The Best Little Whorehouse in Texas; Cannonball Run; Cannonball Run II; The End; Smokey and the Bandit II; Silent Movie)

F. **10** (After Hours; Cheech and Chong's Corsican Brothers; Cheech and Chong's Next Movie; Cheech and Chong's Nice Dreams; FernGully...The Last Rainforest; It Came from Hollywood; Still Smokin'; Things Are Tough All Over; Up in Smoke; Yellowbeard)

G. **9** (Monty Python and the Holy Grail; Life of Brian; Monty Python Live at the Hollywood Bowl; A Fish Called Wanda; And Now For Something Completely Different; Time Bandits; The Secret Policeman's Other Ball; Fierce Creatures)

H. **6** (Any Which Way You Can; Bronco Billy; Every Which Way But Loose; The Gauntlet; The Outlaw Josey Wales; Sudden Impact)

I. **2** (Die Hard with a Vengeance; Pulp Fiction)

J. **4** (Another You; See No Evil, Hear No Evil; Silver Streak; Stir Crazy)

INCREDIBLE MOVIE CHAIN 6: THE FINAL CHAPTER

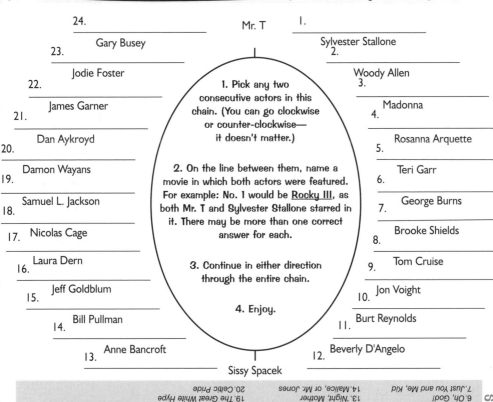

24. _____ Mr. T   1. _____

23. Gary Busey

Sylvester Stallone

22. Jodie Foster   2. _____

Woody Allen

21. James Garner   3. _____

Madonna

20. Dan Aykroyd   4. _____

Rosanna Arquette

19. Damon Wayans   5. _____

Teri Garr

18. Samuel L. Jackson   6. _____

George Burns

17. Nicolas Cage   7. _____

Brooke Shields

16. Laura Dern   8. _____

Tom Cruise

15. Jeff Goldblum   9. _____

Jon Voight

14. Bill Pullman   10. _____

Burt Reynolds

13. Anne Bancroft   11. _____

Beverly D'Angelo

12. _____

Sissy Spacek

1. Pick any two consecutive actors in this chain. (You can go clockwise or counter-clockwise—it doesn't matter.)

2. On the line between them, name a movie in which both actors were featured. For example: No. 1 would be <u>Rocky III</u>, as both Mr. T and Sylvester Stallone starred in it. There may be more than one correct answer for each.

3. Continue in either direction through the entire chain.

4. Enjoy.

ANSWERS

1. Rocky III
2. Bananas
3. Shadows and Fog
4. Desperately Seeking Susan
5. After Hours
6. Oh, God!
7. Just You and Me, Kid
8. Endless Love
9. Mission: Impossible
10. Deliverance
11. Paternity
12. Coal Miner's Daughter
13. 'Night, Mother
14. Malice, or Mr. Jones
15. Independence Day
16. Jurassic Park
17. Wild at Heart
18. Amos & Andrew, or Kiss of Death
19. The Great White Hype
20. Celtic Pride
21. My Fellow Americans
22. Maverick
23. Carny
24. D.C. Cab

BRING OUT YOUR DEAD

Described below are fifteen movies with the word <u>dead</u> in their titles. Identify them all.

1. Radiation turns people into flesh-eating zombies.
2. & 3. Sequels to #1
4. The fifth *Dirty Harry* movie
5. Jeremy Irons plays twin gynecologists.
6. Sam Raimi's directorial debut
7. Robin Williams plays an English teacher.
8. Christopher Walken can predict people's fate just by touching them.
9. Sam Neill and Nicole Kidman battle a psycho on their yacht.
10. Kenneth Branagh's follow-up to *Henry V*
11. Rik Mayall from *The Young Ones* plays Phoebe Cates's obnoxious imaginary friend.
12. Through fancy editing, Steve Martin "stars" with Bogart and Cagney.
13. Joe Piscopo battles reanimated criminals.
14. Sixth *Nightmare on Elm Street* movie
15. John Cusack pines for his ex-girlfriend while falling for the French girl next door.

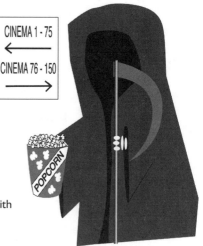

CINEMA 1 - 75

CINEMA 76 - 150

POPCORN

Hollywood Wedding Album

The twenty sets of actors listed below were "married" in Hollywood-movie wedding ceremonies. Identify all the movies in which their characters tied the knot, or we'll make you do the stinkin' Bunny Hop for an hour.

1. Ryan O'Neal and Ali MacGraw
2. Julia Roberts and Dylan McDermott
3. Talia Shire and Gianni Russo
4. Goldie Hawn and Albert Brooks
5. Elizabeth Taylor and Don Taylor
6. Annabella Sciorra and Ron Eldard
7. Tom Hanks and Tawny Kitaen
8. Carrie Fisher and Bruno Kirby
9. George Lazenby and Diana Rigg
10. Miss Piggy and Kermit the Frog
11. Jennifer Jason Leigh and Taylor Negron
12. Meg Ryan and Alec Baldwin
13. Charles Grodin and Jeannie Berlin
14. Kevin Bacon and Elizabeth McGovern
15. Jack Lemmon and Ann-Margret
16. Cary Elwes and Robin Wright
17. Howard Keel and Jane Powell
18. John Savage and Rutanya Alda
19. Julie Andrews and Christopher Plummer
20. Dudley Moore and Ann Reinking and Amy Irving

CASABLANCA, Reel 1

IT'S A WONDERFUL LIFE, REEL

R3, CAN'T STOP THE MUSIC

ANSWERS

1. Love Story
2. Steel Magnolias
3. The Godfather
4. Private Benjamin
5. Father of the Bride
6. True Love
7. Bachelor Party
8. When Harry Met Sally
9. On Her Majesty's Secret Service
10. The Muppets Take Manhattan
11. Easy Money
12. Prelude to a Kiss
13. The Heartbreak Kid
14. She's Having a Baby
15. Grumpy Old Men
16. The Princess Bride
17. Seven Brides for Seven Brothers
18. The Deer Hunter
19. The Sound of Music
20. Micki and Maude

FILM CHARACTERS 101

This one's a cinch! Name the movies that contained these characters, then name the actors who played them. (Note: In the case of characters who appeared in sequels, name the first movie in the series)

_____ 1. Norman Bates

_____ 2. George Bailey

_____ 3. Terry Malloy

_____ 4. Scarlett O'Hara

_____ 5. Luke Skywalker

_____ 6. Rick Blaine

_____ 7. Norma Desmond

_____ 8. R. P. McMurphy

_____ 9. Dorothy Gale

_____ 10. Ratso Rizzo

_____ 11. Maria Von Trapp

_____ 12. Travis Bickle

_____ 13. Mrs. Robinson

_____ 14. "Fast Eddie" Felson

_____ 15. "Popeye" Doyle

_____ 16. Cody Jarrett

_____ 17. Sugar Kane

_____ 18. Charles Foster Kane

_____ 19. Tony Manero

_____ 20. Margo Channing

_____ 21. Harry Callahan

_____ 22. Rufus T. Firefly

_____ 23. Axel Foley

_____ 24. Sarah Conner

_____ 25. Dr. Frank N. Furter

_____ 26. Jim Stark

_____ 27. Ethan Edwards

_____ 28. Bluto Blutarsky

_____ 29. Alvy Singer

_____ 30. Hannibal Lechter

THE NAME IN THE TITLE

Name the actor or actors referred to in the movie titles below. Example: #1 would be Robert De Niro since he plays the taxi driver mentioned in the title.

1. *Taxi Driver*
2. *The Witches of Eastwick*
3. *The Wild One*
4. *Urban Cowboy*
5. *Blade Runner*
6. *The Man Without a Face*
7. *The Graduate*
8. *Ghost*
9. *The American President*
10. *My Fair Lady*
11. *Drugstore Cowboy*
12. *Birdman of Alcatraz*
13. *Cadillac Man*
14. *The Juror*
15. *The Falcon and the Snowman*
16. *Tin Men*
17. *Steel Magnolias*
18. *Spies Like Us*
19. *Housesitter*
20. *Legal Eagles*

21. *The Distinguished Gentleman*
22. *The Good, the Bad, and the Ugly*
23. *The Bodyguard*
24. *The Jerk*
25. *The French Lieutenant's Woman*
26. *A Man Called Horse*
27. *Last Action Hero*
28. *Mr. Wrong*
29. *The Two Jakes*
30. *Desperado*
31. *Bad Boys* (1995)
32. *The Hitcher*
33. *Funny Girl*
34. *Passenger 57*
35. *An Unmarried Woman*
36. *The Doctor*
37. *The Player*
38. *The Rich Man's Wife*
39. *Serial Mom*
40. *The Tall Guy*

ANSWERS

1. Robert De Niro
2. Cher, Michelle Pfeiffer, Susan Sarandon
3. Marlon Brando
4. John Travolta
5. Harrison Ford
6. Mel Gibson
7. Dustin Hoffman
8. Patrick Swayze
9. Michael Douglas
10. Audrey Hepburn
11. Matt Dillon
12. Burt Lancaster
13. Robin Williams
14. Demi Moore
15. Timothy Hutton, Sean Penn
16. Danny DeVito, Richard Dreyfuss
17. Olympia Dukakis, Sally Field, Daryl Hannah, Shirley MacLaine, Dolly Parton, Julia Roberts
18. Dan Aykroyd, Chevy Chase
19. Goldie Hawn
20. Robert Redford, Debra Winger
21. Eddie Murphy
22. Clint Eastwood, Lee Van Cleef, Eli Wallach
23. Kevin Costner
24. Steve Martin
25. Meryl Streep
26. Richard Harris
27. Arnold Schwarzenegger
28. Bill Pullman
29. Jack Nicholson, Harvey Keitel
30. Antonio Banderas
31. Will Smith, Martin Lawrence
32. Rutger Hauer
33. Barbra Streisand
34. Wesley Snipes
35. Jill Clayburgh
36. William Hurt
37. Tim Robbins
38. Halle Berry
39. Kathleen Turner
40. Jeff Goldblum

Bombs Away

Despite their efforts to make only high-quality, intelligent fare, occasionally Hollywood executives accidentally sink money into a stinker. Described below are fifteen movies that performed financially well below their expected take. Name them all.

1. The Bee Gees and Peter Frampton cover the Beatles.
2. Bruce Willis is a smart-mouthed cat burglar.
3. A boy enters the movies with a magical ticket.
4. Two bad songwriters tour the Middle East.
5. An alien duck lands on Earth.
6. An epic retelling of the Johnson County cattle war.
7. The Village People musical.
8. Al Pacino fights the Redcoats.
9. Four-hour epic about the queen of the Nile
10. The hilarious paranoia following the bombing of Pearl Harbor
11. Tom Hanks plays a heartless yuppie.
12. Geena Davis and Matthew Modine are pirates.
13. War toys fight peaceful toys.
14. Dudley Moore is a North Pole elf.
15. Sci-fi extravaganza based on a confusing Frank Herbert book

INCREDIBLE MOVIE CHAIN 7: A NEW BEGINNING

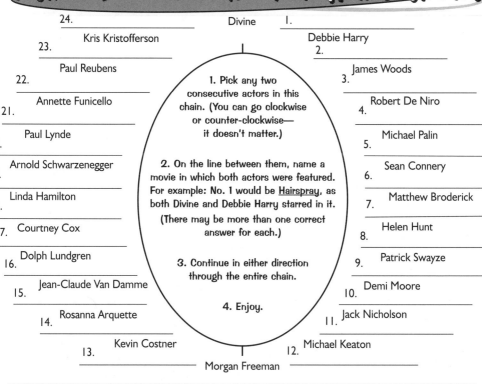

24. _____ Divine 1. _____

23. Kris Kristofferson Debbie Harry

Paul Reubens 2. _____

22. _____ James Woods
3. _____

Annette Funicello Robert De Niro

21. _____ 4. _____

Paul Lynde Michael Palin

20. _____ 5. _____

Arnold Schwarzenegger Sean Connery

19. _____ 6. _____

Linda Hamilton Matthew Broderick

18. _____ 7. _____

17. Courtney Cox Helen Hunt
8. _____

Dolph Lundgren Patrick Swayze

16. _____ 9. _____

Jean-Claude Van Damme Demi Moore

15. _____ 10. _____

Rosanna Arquette Jack Nicholson

14. _____ 11. _____

Kevin Costner Michael Keaton

13. _____ 12. _____

Morgan Freeman

1. Pick any two consecutive actors in this chain. (You can go clockwise or counter-clockwise—it doesn't matter.)

2. On the line between them, name a movie in which both actors were featured. For example: No. 1 would be <u>Hairspray</u>, as both Divine and Debbie Harry starred in it. (There may be more than one correct answer for each.)

3. Continue in either direction through the entire chain.

4. Enjoy.

HELL'S SMORGASBORD

Match each actor with the "food item" that he or she devoured in a movie, then name the respective movies. Those who can't successfully complete this quiz should gnaw on an old tire.

1. A cockroach
2. Dog excrement
3. Lobster shell
4. Canned dog food
5. A shoe
6. A human cheek
7. "Soylent Green"
8. Fifty hard-boiled eggs
9. Tropical fish
10. Stir-fried lamb testicles
11. A ratburger
12. Jell-O from a cafeteria line
13. A deer (raw)
14. Worms mixed with various condiments
15. Human placenta

A. David Naughton
B. Charlton Heston
C. Chevy Chase
D. Samantha Eggar
E. John Belushi
F. Kevin Kline
G. Charlie Chaplin
H. Robin Williams
I. Daryl Hannah
J. Divine
K. Robert De Niro
L. Paul Newman
M. Nicolas Cage
N. Sylvester Stallone
O. Mel Gibson

ANSWERS

1. M. *Vampire's Kiss*
2. J. *Pink Flamingos*
3. I. *Splash*
4. O. *The Road Warrior*
5. G. *The Gold Rush*
6. K. *Cape Fear*
7. B. *Soylent Green*
8. L. *Cool Hand Luke*
9. F. *A Fish Called Wanda*
10. C. *Funny Farm*
11. N. *Demolition Man*
12. E. *National Lampoon's Animal House*
13. A. *An American Werewolf in London*
14. H. *Jack*
15. D. *The Brood*

Cinematic Title Halves

Put the same word before or after all three words in each of the twenty groups listed below and you'll get three different two-word movie titles. For example, the answer to #1 would be Baby (for <u>Baby Boom</u>, <u>Pretty Baby</u>, and <u>Rosemary's Baby</u>). Identify the nineteen other words that would complete the rest of the titles.

1. Boom, Pretty, Rosemary's
2. Lone, Wars, Flaming
3. Atlantic, Fat, Open
4. Body, Impact, Indemnity
5. House, Bachelor, Girl
6. Orpheus, Narcissus, Beauty
7. Detroit, Zhivago, No
8. Grit, Lies, Stories
9. Guns, Forever, Einstein
10. Round, Cowboy, Express

11. Gun, Hat, Secret
12. Anxiety, Noon, Society
13. Madison, Jack, Bronco
14. Trouble, Business, Shines
15. Midnight, Delancey, Miller's
16. Lovers, School, Indian
17. Attraction, Beauty, Instinct
18. Forget, Blues, Texas
19. Free, Yesterday, First
20. Simple, Feast, First

Pretty Baby

Baby Boom

Rosemary's Baby

CINEMATIC COMMONALITIES

What do the four movies in each group have in common?

1. *A Boy and His Dog*
   Alive
   Delicatessen
   The Texas Chainsaw Massacre

2. *Friday the 13th*
   Point Break
   Killing Zoe
   The Phantom of the Opera

3. *Untamed Heart*
   That Was Then, This Is Now
   Fargo
   Purple Rain

4. Robin Williams in *Awakenings*
   Harrison Ford in *The Fugitive*
   Kevin Costner in *Robin Hood: Prince of Thieves*
   Steve Martin in *Grand Canyon*

5. *The Pink Panther*
   Ruthless People
   City Slickers
   Grease

6. *Turbulence*
   Die Hard 2
   The Buddy Holly Story
   Fearless

7. *Grumpy Old Men*
   A River Runs Through It
   Jaws
   On Golden Pond

8. *Sunset Boulevard*
   Double Indemnity
   Forget Paris
   Citizen Kane

9. *Marathon Man*
   Compromising Positions
   Little Shop of Horrors
   The In-Laws

10. *Blue in the Face*
    Get Crazy
    Faraway, So Close
    One Trick Pony

11. *Top Gun*
    Caddyshack
    Footloose
    Over the Top

12. *Ordinary People*
    It's a Wonderful Life
    Down and Out in Beverly Hills
    Meet John Doe

ANSWERS

1. Movies that feature cannibalism

2. Movies in which characters wear masks

3. Movies set in Minneapolis

4. All four actors sported beards at some point in each movie.

5. Movies with animated opening titles

6. Movies that contain a plane crash

7. Movies in which at least one character goes fishing

8. Movies in which the story is told in flashback

9. Movies that have a dentist character

10. Movies that feature Lou Reed

11. Movies that contain a song by Kenny Loggins

12. Movies in which a character attempts suicide

INCREDIBLE INVERSE MOVIE CHAIN

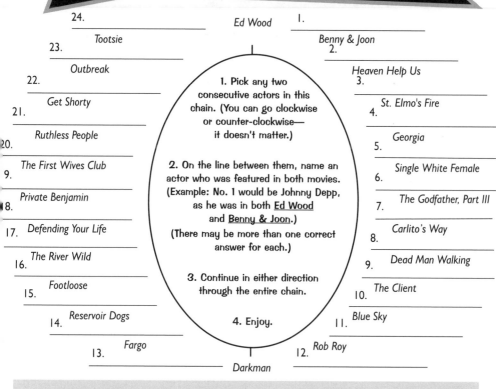

24. _____   Ed Wood   1. _____

23.   Tootsie   Benny & Joon   2. _____

22. _____   Outbreak   Heaven Help Us   3. _____

21. _____   Get Shorty   St. Elmo's Fire   4. _____

20. _____   Ruthless People   Georgia   5. _____

19. _____   The First Wives Club   Single White Female   6. _____

18. _____   Private Benjamin   The Godfather, Part III   7. _____

17. _____   Defending Your Life   Carlito's Way   8. _____

16. _____   The River Wild   Dead Man Walking   9. _____

15. _____   Footloose   The Client   10. _____

14. _____   Reservoir Dogs   Blue Sky   11. _____

13. _____   Fargo   Rob Roy   12. _____

Darkman

1. Pick any two consecutive actors in this chain. (You can go clockwise or counter-clockwise—it doesn't matter.)

2. On the line between them, name an actor who was featured in both movies. (Example: No. 1 would be Johnny Depp, as he was in both __Ed Wood__ and __Benny & Joon__.) (There may be more than one correct answer for each.)

3. Continue in either direction through the entire chain.

4. Enjoy.

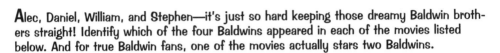

Name That Baldwin

Alec, Daniel, William, and Stephen—it's just so hard keeping those dreamy Baldwin brothers straight! Identify which of the four Baldwins appeared in each of the movies listed below. And for true Baldwin fans, one of the movies actually stars two Baldwins.

_____ 1. *Sliver*

_____ 2. *Last Exit to Brooklyn*

_____ 3. *Beetlejuice*

_____ 4. *Knight Moves*

_____ 5. *Alice*

_____ 6. *Flatliners*

_____ 7. *Posse*

_____ 8. *Harley Davidson and the Marlboro Man*

_____ 9. *Miami Blues*

_____ 10. *Three of Hearts*

_____ 11. *Car 54, Where Are You?*

_____ 12. *The Usual Suspects*

_____ 13. *Born on the Fourth of July*

_____ 14. *Great Balls of Fire*

_____ 15. *Internal Affairs*

_____ 16. *The Shadow*

_____ 17. *Threesome*

_____ 18. *Working Girl*

_____ 19. *Backdraft*

_____ 20. *Glengarry Glen Ross*

THE END OF THE WORLD IS NIGH!

Described below are movies about the end of the world as we know it. Identify them all, then go hide in your bomb shelter until the Emergency Broadcast System says it's okay to come out.

1. Stanley Kubrick's comedy featuring three roles for Peter Sellers.
2. Basically a serious version of #1, with Henry Fonda as president.
3. Charlton Heston fends off zombies in this remake of *I Am Legend*.
4. Mel Gibson fights bad guys for gasoline.
5. Don Johnson and a talking mutt search for food and women.
6. A comet crashes on Earth killing all but a half dozen people.
7. The war between man and machine is fought in the past by a cyborg and a liquid metal creature.
8. All the Earth except Australia has been contaminated by nuclear war, and they're next.
9. A crack team of underwater oil workers meet liquid creatures and prevent a tidal wave from destroying the planet.
10. Zombies trap a small band of survivors in a shopping mall.
11. A young man inadvertently hears the world will end on a pay phone.
12. Bizarre French film in which a circus performer must avoid being cannibalized by the hungry patrons at a hotel.
13. The polar ice caps have melted and there is no land.
14. Russians and Americans make a joint effort to explore strange phenomena in space, but are divided when Cold War tensions flare on Earth.
15. TV movie in which WWIII hits Lawrence, Kansas.

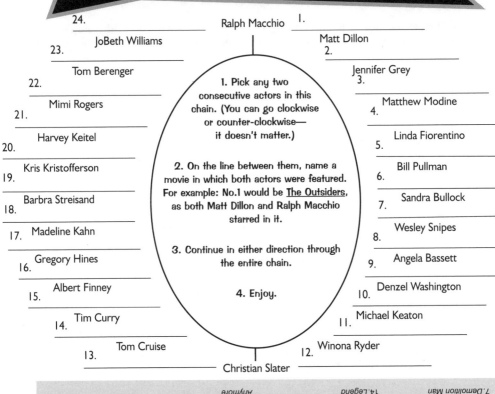

WHOOPEE! ANOTHER INCREDIBLE MOVIE CHAIN

Ralph Macchio — 1.

Matt Dillon — 2.

Jennifer Grey — 3.

Matthew Modine — 4.

Linda Fiorentino — 5.

Bill Pullman — 6.

Sandra Bullock — 7.

Wesley Snipes — 8.

Angela Bassett — 9.

Denzel Washington — 10.

Michael Keaton — 11.

Winona Ryder — 12.

Christian Slater — 13.

Tom Cruise — 14.

Tim Curry — 15.

Albert Finney — 16.

Gregory Hines — 17.

Madeline Kahn — 18.

Barbra Streisand — 19.

Kris Kristofferson — 20.

Harvey Keitel — 21.

Mimi Rogers — 22.

Tom Berenger — 23.

JoBeth Williams — 24.

1. Pick any two consecutive actors in this chain. (You can go clockwise or counter-clockwise—it doesn't matter.)

2. On the line between them, name a movie in which both actors were featured. For example: No.1 would be <u>The Outsiders</u>, as both Matt Dillon and Ralph Macchio starred in it.

3. Continue in either direction through the entire chain.

4. Enjoy.

ANSWERS

1. The Outsiders
2. Bloodhounds of Broadway
3. Wind
4. Vision Quest
5. The Last Seduction
6. While You Were Sleeping
7. Demolition Man
8. Waiting to Exhale
9. Malcolm X
10. Much Ado About Nothing
11. Beetlejuice
12. Heathers
13. Interview with the Vampire
14. Legend
15. Annie
16. Wolfen
17. History of the World, Part 1
18. What's Up, Doc?
19. A Star is Born
20. Alice Doesn't Live Here Anymore
21. Monkey Trouble
22. Someone to Watch Over Me
23. The Big Chill, or Dogs of War
24. Teachers

Oddball Gangs of Misfits

What could be more inspiring than watching a ragtag group of misfit underdogs band together to save the day? Described below are twenty movies about oddball gangs laying waste to stuffed-shirt authority figures. Name them all.

1. Bill Murray counsels the CITs at Camp Northstar.

2. Walter Matthau gets his daughter to pitch for this Little League baseball team.

3. The Delta House disrupts the homecoming parade. Take that, Dean Wormer!

4. Elliott Gould and Donald Sutherland are surgeons in Korea who thumb their noses at their superiors.

5. It's The Slobs vs. The Snobs in this classic golf comedy.

6. Burt Reynolds and other prisoners challenge the guards to a football game.

7. Steve Guttenberg and a band of police recruits put a stop to crime in the streets.

8. Mental patients Michael Keaton, Christopher Lloyd, and Peter Boyle leave the institution and roam New York City—with hilarious results!

9. A group of lovable midgets capture a boy and travel through the centuries with him.

10. A farmboy, a smuggler, a princess, an old warrior, two robots, and a Wookie fight an evil Empire.

11. Emilio Estevez coaches a peewee hockey team.

12. Richard Lewis, Louie Anderson, and other comedians are former Boy Scouts reunited in the wilderness.

13. Clint Eastwood leads a bunch of green troops into Grenada.

14. A band of kids look for pirate treasure and get chased around by Anne Ramsey.

15. Kelsey Grammer commands a wacky fleet of losers on a beat-up old submarine.

16. Telly Savalas, Charles Bronson, and ten others are criminals fighting the good fight in WWII.

17. Bill Murray leads an invasion into Czechoslovakia.

18. Harvey Keitel, Tim Roth, and Steve Buscemi flub a jewel heist.

19. John Candy coaches a Jamaican bobsled team.

20. Tim Matheson and his dumb college chums compete in a river raft race.

INCREDIBLE MOVIE CHAIN 10

24. _____ Kristy McNichol 1. _____

23. Tatum O'Neal _____ Mark Hamill

22. Madeline Kahn _____ 2. _____

21. Cybill Shepherd _____ Annie Potts 3. _____

20. William Hurt _____ Eric Roberts 4. _____

19. Lee Marvin _____ Jon Voight 5. _____

18. Jane Fonda _____ Faye Dunaway 6. _____

17. Jack Lemmon _____ Peter O'Toole 7. _____

16. Burgess Meredith _____ Barbara Hershey 8. _____

15. Laurence Olivier _____ Keanu Reeves 9. _____

14. Dustin Hoffman _____ Winona Ryder 10. _____

13. F. Murray Abraham _____ Jeff Daniels 11. _____

12. Ray Liotta _____

Tom Hulce

1. Pick any two consecutive actors in this chain. (You can go clockwise or counter-clockwise— it doesn't matter.)

2. On the line between them, name a movie in which both actors were featured. For example: No.1 would be <u>The Night the Lights Went out in Georgia</u>, as both Kristy McNichol and Mark Hamill were in it.

3. Continue in either direction through the entire chain.

4. Enjoy.

TIME AND AGAIN

Match the musical artists with the songs they recorded with <u>time</u> in the title.

1. "Time Has Come Today"
2. "Big Time"
3. "Time in a Bottle"
4. "Time Flies"
5. "Time Is on My Side"
6. "Time Heals"
7. "Do That to Me One More Time"
8. "(I've Had) the Time of My Life"
9. "Love Takes Time"
10. "First Time Ever I Saw Your Face
11. "Three Times a Lady"
12. "Every Time You Go Away"
13. "Party All the Time"
14. "Good Times Roll"
15. "Only Time Will Tell"
16. "Second Time Around"
17. "Haven't Got Time for the Pain"
18. "Good Time Charlie's Got the Blues"
19. "Take Your Time (Do It Right)"
20. "Give Me Just a Little More Time"
21. "The Longest Time"
22. "It's Going to Take Some Time"
23. "Time Won't Let Me"
24. "If I Could Turn Back Time"
25. "Feels Like the First Time"

A. The Captain and Tennille
B. The Rolling Stones
C. The Carpenters
D. Tears for Fears
E. Asia
F. The Outsiders
G. Billy Joel
H. Danny O'Keefe
I. Cher
J. The Chamber Brothers
K. Eddie Murphy
L. Paul Young
M. Mariah Carey
N. Jim Croce
O. Foreigner
P. Shalamar
Q. Carly Simon
R. The S.O.S. Band
S. The Commodores
T. Todd Rundgren
U. Peter Gabriel
V. Chairmen of the Board
W. Bill Medley and Jennifer Warnes
X. Roberta Flack
Y. The Cars

FANCY BAND NAMES

Described in the left column are twenty band names. On the right are twenty songs sung by those respective bands. First figure out the band names, then match them with their respective songs.

1. A river in Hades
2. Mad scientist in *Barbarella*
3. Spanish for "the wolves"
4. Weird-looking bouffant hairdos
5. Comic book by the Hernandez Bros.
6. German for "Do You Remember?"
7. Sleep state during which one dreams
8. First half of the title of a Russ Meyer Film
9. First book of the Bible
10. What one burns when one works all night
11. Dorothy's dog in *The Wizard of Oz*
12. TV slang for shows featuring shots of people from the neck up
13. A really old fire truck model
14. Its capital is Topeka
15. Desert-dwelling arachnids that sting
16. A novel by Herman Hesse
17. British form of government
18. Highest state in Buddhism
19. Shortened form for carnivorous dinosaur
20. Common handgun model

A. "Hold the Line"
B. "All in My Mind"
C. "Caught Up in You"
D. "And She Was"
E. "La Bamba"
F. "Carry On Wayward Son"
G. "What's the Frequency, Kenneth?"
H. "Tear the Roof Off the Sucker (Give Up the Funk)"
I. "Wind of Change"
J. "Roam"
K. "Keep on Loving You"
L. "Lithium"
M. "Union of the Snake"
N. "Makes No Sense at All"
O. "Beds Are Burning"
P. "Mr. Roboto"
Q. "House of Pain"
R. "Bang a Gong (Get It On)"
S. "Land of Confusion"
T. "Born to Be Wild"

Parental Influence

The fifteen songs listed below all contain references to parents. Match the songs with the artists that recorded them.

1. "Papa Don't Preach"
2. "Mama Can't Buy You Love"
3. "Father Figure"
4. "Mother's Little Helper"
5. "Color Him Father"
6. "Mother and Child Reunion"
7. "Papa Was a Rollin' Stone"
8. "Does Your Mother Know?"
9. "Daddy, Don't You Walk So Fast"
10. "Tell Mama"
11. "Papa's Got a Brand New Bag"
12. "Mama Said"
13. "Daddy's Home"
14. "Mother"
15. "Mama Said Knock You Out"

A. Wayne Newton
B. Danzig
C. Paul Simon
D. James Brown
E. L. L. Cool J
F. Jermaine Jackson
G. Elton John
H. The Shirelles
I. George Michael
J. The Winstons
K. Madonna
L. The Temptations
M. Etta James
N. Abba
O. The Rolling Stones

MOM — CLEAN YOUR ROOM!

DAD — DO YOUR HOMEWORK!

ANSWERS

1. K   6. C   11. D   14. B
2. G   7. L   12. H   15. E
3. I   8. N   13. F
4. O   9. A
5. J   10. M

NUMBERS RACKET

Complete the song titles below by inserting the appropriate numbers.

1. The Doors' "Love Me ____ Times"
2. The Plimsouls' "A ____ Miles Away"
3. The Commodores' "____ Times a Lady"
4. Tommy Tutone's "____/Jenny"
5. The Stray Cats' "(She's) Sexy + ____"
6. The Byrds' "____ Miles High"
7. Zager & Evans' "In the Year ____"
8. Sam Cooke's "Only ____"
9. ? and the Mysterians' "____ Tears"
10. Kiss' "Christine ____"
11. The Osmonds' "____ Bad Apple"
12. Paul Simon's "____ Ways to Leave Your Lover"
13. Eddie Money's "____ Tickets to Paradise"
14. The Chiffons' "____ Fine Day"
15. The Beatles' "____ Days a Week"
16. The Fixx's "Saved By ____"
17. Wilson Pickett's "____ (Soulville, U.S.A.)"
18. The Vogues' "____ O' Clock World"
19. Gary U. S. Bonds's "Quarter to ____"
20. Brewer & Shipley's "____ Toke Over the Line"

21. Paul Hardcastle's "____"
22. Pete Wingfield's "____ With a Bullet"
23. The Four Seasons' "December, ____ (Oh, What a Night)"
24. Nena's "____ Luftballons"
25. INXS' "The ____ Thing"
26. Lou Christie's "____ Faces Have I"
27. Gene McDaniels's "____ Pounds of Clay"
28. Duane Eddy's "____ Miles of Bad Road"

MUSICAL NICKNAMES

Identify the musical legends for whom these nicknames were created.

1. The Fab Four
2. The King of Rock n' Roll
3. The Material Girl
4. The Chairman of the Board
5. The Boss
6. The Queen of Soul
7. The Man in Black
8. The Grandfather of Punk
9. The Thin White Duke
10. The Queen of Disco
11. The Divine Miss M
12. Slowhand
13. The Killer
14. Satchmo
15. The King of Pop
16. Pearl
17. The Motor City Madman
18. The Glimmer Twins
19. The Hardest Working Man In Show Business
20. The Velvet Fog

ANSWERS

1. The Beatles
2. Elvis Presley
3. Madonna
4. Frank Sinatra
5. Bruce Springsteen
6. Aretha Franklin
7. Johnny Cash
8. Iggy Pop
9. David Bowie
10. Donna Summer
11. Bette Midler
12. Eric Clapton
13. Jerry Lee Lewis
14. Louis Armstrong
15. Michael Jackson
16. Janis Joplin
17. Ted Nugent
18. Mick Jagger and Keith Richards
19. James Brown
20. Mel Torme

I Want My Music Videos

The following are descriptions of images from music videos you might have seen in the early days of MTV. Name the song and artist for which these unforgettable images were forever captured on video.

1. Woman falls for an animated race car driver
2. Feisty singer defies Cap'n Lou Albano, dances in the street
3. When the singer walks, the sidewalk lights up.
4. Five showgirl waterskiers wave to the camera.
5. Dropped cigar ashes decide a pool game
6. Martian knocking on door viewed through a peephole
7. Teenage boy tells angry dad, "I wanna rock," then blasts Dad out the window with the awesome power of one guitar chord
8. Singer's face is projected onto a moving highway
9. Singer puts ring on a bride's finger; draws blood
10. Paulina Porizkova sits in a chair and cries.
11. Singer, dressed as a reporter, interviews a suicidal woman on a building ledge
12. Singer's face ironically superimposed on face of robot
13. Einstein look-alike plays a violin
14. Cross-eyed woman shoots beer can out of cowboy's hand
15. Bumper cars slam into both sides of the singer's head
16. An armadillo runs in front of an oil well.
17. Robotic arm slaps mannequin's head into a table
18. Singing head emerges from a pot of baked beans
19. Scantily clad woman topples sumo wrestler
20. Medieval characters, including a midget, dance around a Maypole

SOLO ACTS

At the right are twenty pop songs of the last twenty years. Each one was sung by a solo artist who was previously in a band. For each song, name the artist and the band he or she was in before hitting it big as a solo act.

_____ _____	1. "The Boys of Summer"
_____ _____	2. "Against All Odds"
_____ _____	3. "Let My Love Open the Door"
_____ _____	4. "The Glory of Love"
_____ _____	5. "Heaven Is a Place on Earth"
_____ _____	6. "Fortress Around Your Heart"
_____ _____	7. "Come as You Are"
_____ _____	8. "Walk on the Wild Side"
_____ _____	9. "Dancing on the Ceiling"
_____ _____	10. "Crazy Train"
_____ _____	11. "Nuthin' But a 'G' Thang"
_____ _____	12. "Dyslexic Heart"
_____ _____	13. "My Prerogative"
_____ _____	14. "Midnight Blue"
_____ _____	15. "Human Behavior"
_____ _____	16. "Big Log"
_____ _____	17. "The Old Man Is Down the Road"
_____ _____	18. "Emotion in Motion"
_____ _____	19. "Just a Gigolo/I Ain't Got Nobody"
_____ _____	20. "Edge of Seventeen"

ANSWERS

1. Don Henley, The Eagles
2. Phil Collins, Genesis
3. Pete Townshend, The Who
4. Peter Cetera, Chicago
5. Belinda Carlisle, The Go-Gos
6. Sting, The Police
7. Peter Wolf, The J. Geils Band
8. Lou Reed, The Velvet Underground
9. Lionel Richie, The Commodores
10. Ozzy Osbourne, Black Sabbath
11. Dr. Dre, N.W.A.
12. Paul Westerberg, The Replacements
13. Bobby Brown, New Edition
14. Lou Gramm, Foreigner
15. Björk, The Sugarcubes
16. Robert Plant, Led Zeppelin
17. John Fogerty, Creedence Clearwater Revival
18. Ric Ocasek, The Cars
19. David Lee Roth, Van Halen
20. Stevie Nicks, Fleetwood Mac

EYES ON THE PRIZE

Each of the artists listed below has had a famous song with the word <u>eye</u> in the title. Name the songs, then donate your eyes to science.

1. Kim Carnes
2. The Eagles
3. Survivor
4. Daryl Hall and John Oates
5. Van Morrison
6. Billy Idol
7. Peter Gabriel
8. Sheena Easton
9. Robert John
10. The Guess Who
11. Crystal Gayle
12. Dr. Hook
13. Frankie Valli
14. The Platters
15. Bob Welch
16. Sugarloaf
17. The Alan Parsons Project
18. The Flamingos
19. Eric Carmen
20. Elton John
21. Jackson Browne
22. Bobby Vee
23. The Grass Roots
24. Go West
25. Night Ranger

Song Title Clones

What do Fleetwood Mac and Starship have in common? They each recorded a different song entitled "Sara." Below are more artists who shared the same title for different songs. Name as many of the shared song titles as you can.

1. David Bowie and Irene Cara
2. Patsy Cline and Seal
3. T'Pau and Huey Lewis & the News
4. U2 and Shadows of Knight
5. R.E.M. and Sly & the Family Stone
6. Jefferson Airplane and Queen
7. The Time and Steve Miller Band
8. ELO and The Animals
9. Kenny Rogers and Little River Band
10. Crosby, Stills & Nash and Madness
11. Madonna and The Association
12. Def Leppard and Ringo Starr
13. Tears for Fears and The Go-Gos
14. Roberta Flack and Bad Company
15. Boston and Fine Young Cannibals
16. Earth, Wind, and Fire and The Manhattans
17. Nu Shooz and Stevie Nicks
18. Barry Manilow and Bob Seger
19. Aerosmith and The Four Seasons
20. Del Shannon and Bon Jovi

ANSWERS

1. "Fame"
2. "Crazy"
3. "Heart and Soul"
4. "Gloria"
5. "Stand"
6. "Somebody to Love"
7. "Jungle Love"
8. "Don't Bring Me Down"
9. "Lady"
10. "Our House"
11. "Cherish"
12. "Photograph"
13. "Head Over Heels"
14. "Feel Like Makin' Love"
15. "Don't Look Back"
16. "Shining Star"
17. "I Can't Wait"
18. "Even Now"
19. "Rag Doll"
20. "Runaway"

THESPIAN ELVIS

Match the Elvis Presley movie title with the description of the role he played.

1. Boxer–garage mechanic
2. Inner city doctor
3. Tuna boat fisherman
4. All-girl-dude-ranch employee
5. Convict-turned-rock-star
6. Overworked photographer
7. Navy frogman
8. Unemployed pilot
9. Race car driver wooing Ann-Margret
10. Race car driver wooing Nancy Sinatra
11. Race car driver wooing three different women
12. Riverboat gambler
13. Carnival singer
14. Rock singer in England
15. Gas-station-attendant-turned-singer
16. Millionaire's-son-turned-water-ski-instructor
17. Chaperone for mobster's daughter
18. Soldier stationed in Germany
19. Inheritor of pineapple fortune
20. Movie star visiting the Middle East
21. Trapeze-artist-turned-cliff-diver
22. Rural boy during Civil War
23. Two roles! — A hillbilly and a military man
24. New Orleans night club singer
25. Manager of travelling show in the 1920s

CLAM-BAKE... Gonna have a Clambake.

A. *Girls! Girls! Girls!*
B. *Loving You*
C. *Fun In Acapulco*
D. *Viva Las Vegas*
E. *Clambake*
F. *Spinout*
G. *Kissin' Cousins*
H. *Paradise, Hawaiian Style*
I. *Frankie and Johnny*
J. *Live a Little, Love a Little*
K. *Harum Scarum*
L. *Speedway*
M. *Love Me Tender*
N. *G. I. Blues*
O. *Tickle Me*
P. *The Trouble with Girls*
Q. *Easy Come, Easy Go*
R. *Kid Galahad*
S. *Girl Happy*
T. *Blue Hawaii*
U. *Roustabout*
V. *King Creole*
W. *Double Trouble*
X. *Change of Habit*
Y. *Jailhouse Rock*

HOT TIMES

Part 1: Each of the following musical artists has a famous song with the word <u>fire</u> in the title. Name the songs.

1. Jerry Lee Lewis
2. John Cougar Mellencamp
3. Johnny Cash
4. The Doors
5. Randy Meisner
6. Sanford/Townsend Band
7. Pat Benatar
8. Billy Joel
9. REO Speedwagon
10. Big Country

Part 2: Each of the following musical artists has a famous song with the word <u>hot</u> in the title. Name the songs.

1. Donna Summer
2. Nick Gilder
3. Foreigner
4. Sly & the Family Stone
5. Power Station
6. The Sylvers
7. Robbie Dupree
8. Kool and the Gang
9. Jerry Reed
10. Buster Poindexter

ANSWERS

PART 1
1. "Great Balls of Fire"
2. "Paper in Fire"
3. "Ring of Fire"
4. "Light My Fire"
5. "Hearts on Fire"
6. "Smoke from a Distant Fire"
7. "Fire and Ice"
8. "We Didn't Start the Fire"
9. "Keep the Fire Burning"
10. "Fields of Fire (400 Miles)"

PART 2
1. "Hot Stuff"
2. "Hot Child in The City"
3. "Hot Blooded"
4. "Hot Fun in the Summertime"
5. "Some Like It Hot"
6. "Hot Line"
7. "Hot Rod Hearts"
8. "Too Hot"
9. "When You're Hot, You're Hot"
10. "Hot Hot Hot"

What Is Love, Anyway?

Howard Jones asked it, and many have answered. Below are musical artists who had a hit song with "Love Is . . ." at the beginning of the title. Complete the titles of these artists' "Love Is . . ." songs to answer this age-old question.

1. Andy Gibb
2. Pat Benatar
3. Donnie Iris
4. Roxy Music
5. Sweet
6. John Paul Young
7. Rick Springfield
8. Sting
9. Gary Wright
10. Eurythmics
11. The Troggs
12. England Dan and John Ford Coley
13. The Supremes (two possible answers)

"Love Is _____"
"Love Is _____"
"Love Is _____"
"Love Is _____"
"Love Is _____"
"Love Is _____"
"Love Is _____"
"Love Is _____"
"Love Is _____"
"Love Is _____"
"Love Is _____"
"Love Is _____"
"Love Is _____" or
"Love Is _____"

BEASTS OF BALLADS

Each animal in the right column appeared in the title of a song sung by one of the musical artists in the left column. Match the artists with their corresponding animals, then state the complete titles of the famous animal songs they sang. Each animal is used only once. Happy hunting.

1. Steve Miller
2. Jefferson Airplane
3. Survivor
4. The Beatles
5. Harry Chapin
6. The B-52's
7. Prince
8. Bill Haley and his Comets
9. The Tokens
10. Rick Dees and his Cast of Idiots
11. Led Zeppelin
12. Peter Gabriel
13. The Captain and Tennille
14. Duran Duran
15. The Osmonds
16. Sweet
17. Loudon Wainwright III
18. Elton John
19. Neneh Cherry
20. Heart

A. Alligator
B. Barracuda
C. Muskrat
D. Buffalo
E. Cat
F. Crocodile
G. Dog
H. Dove
I. Duck
J. Eagle
K. Fox
L. Horse
M. Lion
N. Lobster
O. Monkey
P. Rabbit
Q. Skunk
R. Tiger
S. Wolf
T. Walrus

I'M THE OCELOT OF LOVE

Mastery Through Repetition

Listed below are twenty artists who recorded famous songs with repetitive titles (i.e., titles in which the same word is repeated twice). Identify all twenty songs.

1. The Kingsmen
2. Tommy James and the Shondells
3. The Mamas and the Papas
4. The Archies
5. John Parr
6. Naked Eyes
7. Elvis Costello and the Attractions
8. Abba
9. Paula Abdul
10. Thompson Twins
11. Neil Diamond
12. Amy Grant
13. Little Richard
14. 38 Special
15. The Jamies
16. Alive & Kicking
17. The Beau Brummels
18. Gary Puckett and the Union Gap
19. The Dixie Cups
20. Talk Talk

Louie Louie…
Louie Louie…
Louie Louie…
Louie Louie…
Louie Louie…

A Downpour of Hits

Each of the musical artists listed below has recorded a famous song with the word <u>rain</u> in its title. Name them all, then put on your raincoat before you catch your death!

1. The Carpenters
2. Prince
3. B. J. Thomas
4. Neil Sedaka
5. Eddie Rabbitt
6. Oran "Juice" Jones
7. Supertramp
8. John Cougar Mellencamp
9. James Taylor
10. Gordon Lightfoot
11. Brook Benton
12. Nelson
13. Eurythmics
14. The Cascades
15. Kermit the Frog
16. Phil Collins
17. The Weather Girls
18. Dee Clark
19. Bruce Hornsby and the Range
20. Creedence Clearwater Revival (two possible choices)

MAKIN' MUSIC TOGETHER

What do you get when you take two pop music giants and unite them in a recording studio? Super-powered hits, that's what! Name the songs these musical collaborators recorded together.

1. Queen and David Bowie
2. Paul McCartney and Stevie Wonder
3. Kenny Rogers and Dolly Parton
4. Bryan Adams and Tina Turner
5. Barbra Streisand and Neil Diamond
6. Run–D.M.C. and Aerosmith
7. Crystal Gayle and Eddie Rabbitt
8. Stevie Nicks and Tom Petty and the Heartbreakers
9. Joe Cocker and Jennifer Warnes
10. Elton John and Kiki Dee
11. Diana Ross and Lionel Richie
12. Eurythmics and Aretha Franklin
13. Julio Iglesias and Willie Nelson
14. The Art of Noise and Tom Jones
15. Kenny Loggins and Steve Perry
16. Electric Light Orchestra and Olivia Newton-John
17. The Jacksons and Mick Jagger
18. Mike Reno and Ann Wilson
19. Peabo Bryson and Roberta Flack
20. Paul McCartney and Michael Jackson (two possible choices)

ANSWERS

1. "Under Pressure"
2. "Ebony and Ivory"
3. "Islands in the Stream"
4. "It's Only Love"
5. "You Don't Bring Me Flowers"
6. "Walk This Way"
7. "You and I"
8. "Stop Dragging My Heart Around"
9. "Up Where We Belong"
10. "Don't Go Breaking My Heart"
11. "Endless Love"
12. "Sisters Are Doing It for Themselves"
13. "To All the Girls I've Loved Before"
14. "Kiss"
15. "Don't Fight It"
16. "Xanadu"
17. "State of Shock"
18. "Almost Paradise (Love theme from *Footloose*)"
19. "Tonight, I Celebrate My Love"
20. "Say Say Say" and "The Girl Is Mine"

A ROSE BY ANY OTHER NAME

Has this happened to you? You've heard a song a million times, and you finally decide to buckle down and buy the record, only to find out that the title you'd attached to the song is <u>completely</u> different from the real title. Listed below are some famous songs with their commonly perceived titles (based on prominent or repeated phrases in each song). Correctly identify all of the song titles below.

1. Bob Dylan's "Everybody Must Get Stoned"
2. The Clash's "Stand By Me"
3. Buffalo Springfield's "Stop, Hey, What's That Sound?"
4. The Who's "Teenage Wasteland"
5. Led Zeppelin's "Hey Hey Mama"
6. Howard Jones' "Don't Crack Up"
7. Michael Penn's "(I'm Just Looking For) Someone to Dance With"
8. The Greg Kihn Band's "They Don't Write 'Em Like That Anymore"
9. Nirvana's "Hello Hello Hello How Low"
10. LaBelle's "Voulez-Vous Coucher Avec Moi Ce Soir?"
11. David Bowie's "Ground Control to Major Tom"
12. Fleetwood Mac's "Thunder Only Happens When It's Raining"
13. Stevie Wonder's "You Can Feel It All Over"
14. R.E.M's "I'm Sorry"
15. The Beatles' "They're Gonna Crucify Me"

> Personally, my favorite song is Talking Heads' "This Ain't No Party, This Ain't No Disco."*

*Actual Title: "Life During Wartime"

Abra-Ca-Dabra

Each of the musical artists listed below has recorded a song with the word <u>magic</u> in the title. If you name all the songs correctly, we might reveal all of David Copperfield's trade secrets. (Hint: Three of the artists below recorded a song entitled simply "Magic.")

1. The Lovin' Spoonful
2. The Police
3. The Cars
4. Steppenwolf
5. The Who
6. Santana
7. Olivia Newton-John
8. Barry Manilow
9. The Beatles
10. America
11. The Platters
12. Pilot
13. Heart
14. Electric Light Orchestra
15. Peter, Paul and Mary

AMERICA THE MUSICAL

The artists listed below each sang a popular song with the name of a U.S. state or city in its title. Identify the songs.

STATES

1. The Rivieras
2. Ray Charles
3. Mark Lindsay
4. Arrested Development
5. R. Dean Taylor
6. Mountain
7. Crosby, Stills, Nash & Young
8. Lynyrd Skynyrd
9. Neil Diamond
10. The Bee Gees
11. George Strait
12. The Ventures

CITIES

13. Arlo Guthrie
14. Wilbert Harrison
15. Paper Lace
16. Sheryl Crow
17. Elton John
18. Manhattan Transfer
19. Scott McKenzie
20. Dave Loggins
21. Kiss
22. Johnny Rivers
23. Diesel
24. Missing Persons

"Oh, say can you see By the"...um...uh...

DEBUT ALBUMS

The forty album titles listed below were the first full-length efforts of forty different musical artists. Some went on to superstardom, others became answers to trivia questions. Break out your vinyl and name all the artists.

1. *Murmur*
2. *Boy*
3. *Please Please Me*
4. *Licensed to Ill*
5. *Big Science*
6. *Beauty and the Beat*
7. *Bleach*
8. *Yo! Bum Rush the Show!*
9. *My Aim Is True*
10. *For You*
11. *Little Earthquakes*
12. *Wednesday Morning, 3 A.M.*
13. *Outlandos d'Amour*
14. *Are You Experienced?*
15. *Pretties for You*
16. *Speak & Spell*
17. *Freak Out*
18. *Los Angeles*
19. *Kill 'Em All*
20. *England's Newest Hitmakers*
21. *Sorry, Ma, Forgot to Take Out The Trash*
22. *Greetings from Asbury Park, New Jersey*
23. *The Lion and the Cobra*
24. *Psychocandy*
25. *Please Please Please*
26. *Music from the Big Pink*
27. *Surfin' Surfari*
28. *The Piper at the Gates of Dawn*
29. *The Jazz Soul of Little Stevie*
30. *The Kick Inside*
31. *Ten*
32. *I Got Dem Ol' Kosmic Blues Again Mama!*
33. *All Things Must Pass*
34. *Pretty Hate Machine*
35. *Vivid*
36. *One Step Beyond…*
37. *Mellow Gold*
38. *Appetite for Destruction*
39. *Got to Be There*
40. *Telephone Free Landslide Victory*

Dreamy Tunes

Each of the artists below sung a song with the word <u>dream</u> in the title. Correctly identifying all songs may result in one full night of uninterrupted sleep.

1. Gary Wright
2. Debbie Gibson
3. Cheap Trick
4. The Everly Brothers
5. Aerosmith
6. Eurythmics
7. The Moody Blues (two possible choices)
8. Daryl Hall and John Oates
9. Crowded House
10. The Lovin' Spoonful
11. The Electric Prunes
12. The Cranberries
13. Dan Hartman
14. Kenny Nolan
15. Blondie
16. John Lennon
17. The Monkees
18. Roy Orbison (two possible choices)
19. Johnny Hates Jazz
20. Kenny Rogers and Kim Carnes

ANSWERS

1. "Dream Weaver"
2. "Only in My Dreams"
3. "Dream Police"
4. "All I Have to Do Is Dream"
5. "Dream On"
6. "Sweet Dreams (Are Made of This)"
7. "Gemini Dream," or "Your Wildest Dreams"
8. "You Make My Dreams"
9. "Don't Dream It's Over"
10. "Daydream"
11. "I Had Too Much to Dream Last Night"
12. "Dreams"
13. "I Can Dream About You"
14. "I Like Dreamin'"
15. "Dreaming"
16. "#9 Dream"
17. "Daydream Believer"
18. "Dream Baby," or "In Dreams"
19. "Shattered Dreams"
20. "Don't Fall in Love with a Dreamer"

NOVELTY ACTS

The following are descriptions of twenty well-known novelty songs. Identify them all.

1. Ray Stevens's play-by-play about a naked guy

2. Steve Martin salutes a museum exhibit

3. Brian Hyland's tale about a skimpy swimsuit

4. Napoleon XIV rants about being committed.

5. Allen Sherman reads a letter from camp.

6. Kip Addotta rattles off a jillion fish puns.

7. David Seville chants "Ooh-ee-ooh-ah-ah Ting Tang Walla Walla Bing Bang."

8. Bobby Pickett affects a Boris Karloff accent for this dance craze record.

9. Bob and Doug McKenzie share Canadian witticisms with Rush's Geddy Lee.

10. Buckner & Garcia's video-game illness.

11. Chuck Berry's double entendre about "silver bells hanging on a string"

12. Nervous Norvus needs blood after wrecking his car in this 1956 hit.

13. "Fowl" Rick Dees's dance floor abomination

14. Julie Brown sings about a high school tragedy.

15. Jump 'N' the Saddle's tribute to a Stooge

16. Sheb Wooley's close encounter with an alien

17. Comic strip character immortalized by Hollywood Argyles

18. Weird Al Yankovic's parody of Michael Jackson's "Bad"

19. According to Barnes & Barnes, they don't play baseball or wear sweaters.

20. Larry Groce sings about pigging out on unhealthy snacks.

SOMETHING TO DRINK

The fifteen musical acts listed below sang at least one song with a beverage in the title. Name all the songs, then go out and get yourself a malt.

1. The Eagles
2. Jimmy Buffett
3. Snoop Doggy Dogg
4. Squeeze
5. Rupert Holmes
6. Tommy James and the Shondells
7. Hank Williams
8. Looking Glass
9. The Champs
10. Andy Gibb
11. UB40
12. Herman's Hermits
13. The Fireballs
14. Tom T. Hall
15. Tin Tin

Sun Worshippers

The musical acts listed below sang at least one song with the word <u>sun</u> (or a word with sun as its first syllable) in the title. Name all the songs, but don't forget to wear UV protection.

1. Katrina and the Waves
2. Elton John
3. Artists United Against Apartheid
4. a-ha
5. Stevie Wonder
6. John Denver
7. Bobby Hebb
8. Jonathan Edwards
9. The Violent Femmes
10. The Walker Bros.
11. Cream
12. The Sex Pistols
13. The Rivieras
14. Terry Jacks
15. The Animals
16. Bill Withers

BONUS: Name all the Beatles' songs with *sun* in the title (There are four.)

DUMP CITY

Described below are pop songs about getting dumped. Identify them all, then go cry in your beer, you big baby.

1. Leslie Gore loses Johnny to Judy at a doomed soireé.
2. Elvis Presley "dwells" here to "cry away his gloom."
3. Alanis Morissette reminds her ex of the "mess (he) left when (he) went away."
4. Gilbert O'Sullivan decides to leap from a tower after he gets the heave-ho.
5. Daryl Hall and John Oates made this sudden realization in 1976.
6. Michael Jackson nearly weeps at the end of this ballad from *Off the Wall*.
7. Neil Sedaka made this observation in 1962, then pondered it more slowly in 1975.
8. Someday the Everly Brothers might "wear a smile and walk in the sun," but for now they're stuck doing this.
9. The Police warn their beloved "you'll be sorry when I'm dead."
10. She left Kenny Rogers with "four hungry children and a crop in the field."
11. First Gloria Gaynor was "afraid," nay, "petrified," but she handled this break-up with this bit of wisdom.
12. Bananarama's season of lovelessness
13. What Jackie Wilson cries
14. Bobby Vee's plea to his ex-flame's new love
15. All that Ringo Starr has left now that he "realizes (his beloved's) not coming back anymore"

This quiz is so clever it'll make you puke. The following rock 'n' roll bands have recorded at least one rock 'n' roll song with the phrase "rock 'n' roll" (or "rock and roll") in the title. Name 'em all, then check the answers. If you can come up with more songs than are listed here, well, then bully for you!

1. Joan Jett and the Blackhearts
2. Bob Seger (two possible choices)
3. Kiss (two possible choices)
4. The Ramones (two possible choices)
5. Boston
6. Bad Company
7. Billy Joel
8. Electric Light Orchestra
9. Rick Derringer
10. Chuck Berry
11. Danny and the Juniors
12. Spinal Tap
13. Shaun Cassidy
14. The Righteous Brothers
15. The Moody Blues

16. Huey Lewis and the News
17. Ian Dury
18. The Velvet Underground
19. Led Zeppelin
20. Trio

ANSWERS

1. "I Love Rock and Roll"
2. "Old Time Rock 'n' Roll," and "Rock and Roll Never Forgets"
3. "Rock and Roll All Night," and "Let Me Go, Rock 'N' Roll"
4. "Rock 'n' Roll High School," and "Do You Remember Rock 'n' Roll Radio"
5. "Rock & Roll Band"
6. "Rock 'n' Roll Fantasy"
7. "It's Still Rock and Roll to Me"
8. "Rock & Roll Is King"
9. "Rock 'n' Roll Hoochie Koo"
10. "Rock and Roll Music"
11. "Rock 'n' Roll Is Here to Stay"
12. "Rock 'n' Roll Creation"
13. "That's Rock 'n' Roll"
14. "Rock and Roll Heaven"
15. "I'm Just a Singer in a Rock 'n' Roll Band"
16. "Heart of Rock & Roll"
17. "Sex and Drugs and Rock and Roll"
18. "Rock and Roll"
19. "Rock and Roll"
20. "Ich Lieb Den Rock 'n' Roll"

Take the Lead

For each of the bands listed below, name the front man or woman.

1. _____ and the E Street Band
2. _____ and Crazy Horse
3. _____ and the Supremes
4. _____ and the Revolution
5. _____ and the Wailers
6. _____ and the Silver Bullet Band
7. _____ and the News
8. _____ and the Crickets
9. _____ and the Heartbreakers
10. _____ and the Shondells
11. _____ and the Four Seasons
12. _____ and War
13. _____ and the Blackhearts
14. _____ and the All Stars
15. _____ and the Comets
16. _____ and the Rumour
17. _____ and the Attractions
18. _____ and the Miracles
19. _____ and the Vandellas
20. _____ and the Asbury Jukes

21. _____ and the Bluenotes
22. _____ and the Teenagers
23. _____ and the Pips
24. _____ and the MGs
25. _____ and the Dakotas
26. _____ and the Mysterians
27. _____ and the Belmonts
28. _____ and the Imperials
29. _____ and the Furious Five
30. _____ and the Raiders
31. _____ and the Aces
32. _____ and the Famous Flames
33. _____ and the Playboys
34. _____ and Wings
35. _____ and the Mindbenders
36. _____ and the Beaver Brown Band
37. _____ and the Detroit Wheels
38. _____ and the Pharoahs
39. _____ and the First Edition
40. _____ and the Union Gap

EIGHTIES SPELLDOWN

Described below are musical acts from the 1980s, both one-hit wonders and pop veterans. Identify the names of all the acts, then, for a bonus, read down the first letter from each act in numerical order to spell the name of two '80s groups. Important hints: To get the bonus groups, ignore the word "the" if it is the first word in an act's name. Names of individuals should be written just like you'd see them, rather than last name first.

1. This band's lead singer was married to the lead singer of Simple Minds.
2. "True" and "Gold" were their two big hits.
3. Their song "Oh, Yeah" was used in countless movies in the '80s.
4. Known almost as much for their androgynous lead singer as their songs, they sang "I'll Tumble 4 You" and "Do You Really Want to Hurt Me?"
5. They asked the musical question "Don't You Want Me?"
6. He sang the original (but scrapped) theme to *Romancing the Stone*, but he's best known for "Electric Avenue."
7. Their only hit was "Come on Eileen."
8. What Annie Lennox and Dave Stewart were better know as
9. This band claimed everybody's "Working for the Weekend."
10. They sang "Whisper to a Scream (Birds Fly)."

11. He wears his "Sunglasses at Night."
12. They followed up "Relax" with "Two Tribes"
13. Videos from this band's "Reap the Wild Wind" and "Vienna" were early MTV staples.
14. This son of Berry Gordy, Jr. got big help from Michael Jackson on "Somebody's Watching Me."
15. Before "featuring Patty Smyth" was added to end of this band's name, they had minor hits with "Goodbye to You," and "Love's Got A Line on You."
16. Their albums *Business as Usual* and *Cargo* were huge sellers.
17. Their big hit was "Obsession."
18. This band divided briefly into Arcadia and The Power Station in the mid-80s.
19. She recorded an antiwar protest song in both English and German.
20. Every day he writes the book.
21. This rockabilly trio really "rocked this town."
22. Their first big hit was "Holding Back The Years."

ANSWERS

1. (The) Pretenders
2. Spandau Ballet
3. Yello
4. Culture Club
5. (The) Human League
6. Eddy Grant
7. Dexy's Midnight Runners
8. Eurythmics
9. Loverboy
10. Icicle Works
11. Corey Hart
12. Frankie Goes to Hollywood
13. Ultravox
14. Rockwell
15. Scandal
16. Men at Work
17. Animotion
18. Duran Duran
19. Nena
20. Elvis Costello
21. (The) Stray Cats
22. Simply Red

Bonus Band Names: Psychedelic Furs and Madness

UNDER COVER ANGELS

Just like Hollywood's penchant for remaking popular old movies, smart movers in the music biz know redoing a song everyone already knows takes away some of the gamble. Listed below are twenty sets of musical acts. The acts in each set had a hit with the same song. For each set, name the song.

1. Sonny & Cher; UB40 with Chrissie Hynde
2. Lipps, Inc.; Pseudo Echo
3. Brownsville Station; Mötley Crüe
4. Roberta Flack; The Fugees
5. Lynyrd Skynyrd; Will to Power
6. Cat Stevens; Maxi Priest
7. The Strangeloves; Bow Wow Wow
8. Willie Nelson; Pet Shop Boys
9. Otis Redding; Michael Bolton
10. The Five Man Electric Band; Tesla
11. The Righteous Brothers; Daryl Hall and John Oates
12. Little Eva; Grand Funk Railroad; Kylie Minogue
13. Sam & Dave; The Blues Brothers
14. Creedence Clearwater Revival; Ike and Tina Turner
15. The Supremes; Phil Collins
16. Loggins & Messina; Poison
17. Jackie DeShannon; Annie Lennox and Al Green
18. The Marvelettes; The Carpenters
19. Marvin Gaye; Cyndi Lauper
20. Tommy James and the Shondells; Tiffany

Sex, Drugs, and...the Movies

Match the musical artist with the movie in which he or she appeared.

1. David Bowie
2. Bob Dylan
3. Huey Lewis
4. Debbie Harry
5. Ringo Starr
6. Sting
7. Ice Cube
8. Meat Loaf
9. Madonna
10. Rick Nelson
11. Little Richard
12. Cyndi Lauper
13. Ice-T
14. Diana Ross
15. Gene Simmons
16. Mick Jagger
17. Whitney Houston
18. Gregg Allman
19. Alice Cooper
20. Queen Latifah
21. Adam Horovitz (of The Beastie Boys)
22. Isaac Hayes
23. Billy Idol
24. Neil Diamond
25. Tupac Shakur

A. *The Doors*
B. *Waiting to Exhale*
C. *Prince of Darkness*
D. *Vibes*
E. *Rush*
F. *Lost Angels*
G. *The Magic Christian*
H. *Down and Out in Beverly Hills*
I. *New Jack City*
J. *Brimstone and Treacle*
K. *Short Cuts*
L. *Merry Christmas, Mr. Lawrence*
M. *Set it Off*
N. *Juice*
O. *Rio Bravo*
P. *It Could Happen to You*
Q. *Videodrome*
R. *Mahogany*
S. *Evita*
T. *Pat Garrett and Billy the Kid*
U. *Boyz n' the Hood*
V. *The Jazz Singer*
W. *Runaway*
X. *Performance*
Y. *The Rocky Horror Picture Show*

BRITISH-IRISH-SCOTTISH-AUSTRALIAN INVASION

When we think of British bands and musical artisans, we unwashed Americans often lump all acts from England, Scotland, Ireland, Australia, and New Zealand into the mix just because they also speak English. Well, shame on us. Let's right this cultural wrong by correctly identifying the native countries of these musical acts.

1. U2
2. The Bay City Rollers
3. The Kinks
4. Pink Floyd
5. Midnight Oil
6. The Cranberries
7. Simple Minds
8. Depeche Mode
9. The Proclaimers
10. INXS
11. Sheena Easton
12. Men at Work
13. Tears for Fears
14. Sinead O'Connor
15. Enya
16. New Order
17. Nazareth
18. Human League
19. The Little River Band

20. The Clash
21. The Boomtown Rats
22. The Zombies
23. Altered Images
24. Thin Lizzy
25. Dire Straits
26. Air Supply
27. Genesis
28. Squeeze
29. Big Country
30. Donovan
31. The Animals

32. Bananarama
33. Split Enz
34. Van Morrison
35. UB40
36. Roxy Music
37. Rick Springfield
38. AC/DC
39. The Cure
40. Motörhead

SEVENTIES SPELLDOWN

Described below are musical acts from the 1970s. From the clues, identify the names of all the acts, then, for a bonus, read down the first letter from each act in numerical order to spell the name of another '70s group. Important hints: To get the bonus group, ignore the word "the" if it is the first word in an act's name. Names of individuals should be written just like you'd see them, rather than last name first.

1. Their songs for *Saturday Night Fever* made it the best-selling soundtrack ever.

2. What Anni-Frid, Bjorn, Benny, and Agnetha were better known as

3. Hubby played keyboards and wore a hat; wife sang about "love keeping us together,"

4. Had hits with "Boogie Nights" and "Groove Line"

5. This lady sang about "Midnight at the Oasis."

6. Sang "A Horse with No Name," and "Sister Golden Hair"

7. Buffalo Springfield and Crazy Horse were just two of his bands.

8. "One," "Joy To The World," and "Black & White" were three of their hits.

9. "Smiling Faces Sometimes" was a hit for this soul group.

10. Before Eric Carmen sang "All By Myself," he and this group urged us to "Go All the Way"

11. His first name's Harry, but the singer of "Everybody's Talkin'" usually went by this name.

12. He's had hits in the '70s, '80s and '90s, but his first was "Your Song."

13. Recorded the theme to the movie *Car Wash*

14. Everyone wanted to take a ride on their "Love Rollercoaster" in 1975.

15. This disco group consisted of a cop, a cowboy, an Indian, a construction worker, a sailor, and a leather-clad motorcycle guy.

16. They disbanded in 1982, then re-formed in the '90s when "Hell froze over."

17. He asked "Do Ya Think Think I'm Sexy?" then married Rachel Hunter.

18. Tony Orlando and his female background singers recorded "Knock Three Times" under this name.

19. Covered blues standard "Black Betty"

20. They made "Twist and Shout" a hit first in 1962, then sang "Fight the Power Part 1."

21. Urged us to do "The Hustle"

22. Future country band whose first hit was "Kiss You All Over"

A Buncha "Baby"s

Match the musical artists with the songs they recorded that have <u>baby</u> in the title.

1. "Baby, I Love You"
2. "Baby, What a Big Surprise"
3. "Baby Don't Get Hooked on Me"
4. "I'm Your Baby Tonight"
5. "Baby's Got Back"
6. "Cry Like a Baby"
7. "Baby I Love Your Way"
8. "Baby I'm-A Want You"
9. "Sweet Baby James"
10. "Doing It All for My Baby"
11. "Baby Makes Her Blue Jeans Talk"
12. "My Angel Baby"
13. "Baby Come Back"
14. "My Baby Loves Lovin'"
15. "Beach Baby"
16. "Love to Love You Baby"
17. "Maybe Baby"
18. "Baby You're A Rich Man"
19. "Take Good Care of My Baby"
20. "Baby I'm a Star"
21. "Baby Love"
22. "Baby, It's You"
23. "Baby, Now That I've Found You"
24. "Baby, Come to Me"
25. "Rock Me Baby"

A. Huey Lewis and the News
B. Buddy Holly
C. White Plains
D. Player
E. The Beatles
F. Prince
G. Toby Beau
H. The Ronettes
I. Patti Austin with James Ingram
J. The Foundations
K. Sir Mix-A-Lot
L. James Taylor
M. The Supremes
N. Chicago
O. Bobby Vee
P. Whitney Houston
Q. The Box Tops
R. Donna Summer
S. Peter Frampton
T. Dr. Hook
U. David Cassidy
V. Mac Davis
W. First Class
X. The Shirelles
Y. Bread

ANSWERS

25. U	20. F	15. W	10. A	5. K
24. I	19. O	14. C	9. L	4. P
23. J	18. E	13. D	8. Y	3. V
22. X	17. B	12. G	7. S	2. N
21. M	16. R	11. T	6. Q	1. H

NINETIES-PALOOZA

Listed below is a sampling of songs from the '90s. Identify the artists who sang them.

1. "Cherub Rock"
2. "Jump Around"
3. "Mr. Jones"
4. "Gin and Juice"
5. "Live Forever"
6. "Cannonball"
7. "Connection"
8. "You Mean the World to Me"
9. "Buddy Holly"
10. "Jeremy"
11. "Sheila Na Gig"
12. "Mmmm Mmmm Mmmm Mmmm"
13. "Longview"
14. "I Alone"
15. "Stupid Girl"
16. "Vasoline"
17. "Closer"
18. "Runaway Train"
19. "Shine"
20. "Come to My Window"

21. "Black Hole Sun"
22. "Loser"
23. "Are You Gonna Go My Way?"
24. "Gangsta's Paradise"
25. "Heart-Shaped Box"
26. "Don't Turn Around"
27. "Seether"
28. "Motownphilly"
29. "Only Wanna Be with You"
30. "Cut Your Hair"
31. "My Lovin' (You're Never Gonna Get It)"
32. "Friends In Low Places"
33. "Doll Parts"
34. "Hey Jealousy"
35. "Crucify"
36. "Peaches"
37. "She Talks to Angels"
38. "Sick of Myself"
39. "Lucas with the Lid Off"
40. "O.P.P."

ANSWERS

1. Smashing Pumpkins
2. House of Pain
3. Counting Crows
4. Snoop Doggy Dogg
5. Oasis
6. The Breeders
7. Elastica
8. Toni Braxton
9. Weezer
10. Pearl Jam
11. PJ Harvey
12. Crash Test Dummies
13. Green Day
14. Live
15. Garbage
16. Stone Temple Pilots
17. Nine Inch Nails
18. Soul Asylum
19. Collective Soul
20. Melissa Etheridge
21. Soundgarden
22. Beck
23. Lenny Kravitz
24. Coolio
25. Nirvana
26. Ace of Base
27. Veruca Salt
28. Boyz II Men
29. Hootie and the Blowfish
30. Pavement
31. En Vogue
32. Garth Brooks
33. Hole
34. Gin Blossoms
35. Tori Amos
36. The Presidents of the United States of America
37. The Black Crowes
38. Matthew Sweet
39. Lucas
40. Naughty By Nature

Test Your General Pop Culture IQ!

POP CULTURE THREESOMES

What do the three things in each set below have in common? Be as specific as possible.

1. *Turner and Hooch, K-9, Top Dog*

2. Huckle Cat, Lowly Worm, Sgt. Murphy

3. *The Far Side, The Family Circus, Dennis the Menace*

4. Flub-A-Dub, Phineas T. Bluster, Dilly Dally

5. Gladys Kravitz, Millie Helper, Stanley Roper

6. America, Asia, Europe

7. Richard Burton, Eddie Fisher, Michael Todd

8. *His Girl Friday, The Mean Season, Absence of Malice*

9. "Brother Louie" by Stories, "Society's Child" by Janis Ian, "Half-Breed" by Cher

10. *Magnum P.I., Simon and Simon, The A Team*

11. Opus, Chilly Willy, Tennessee Tuxedo

12. Tomy, Marx, Galoob

13. Alderaan, Yavin, Dantooine

14. Goofy Grape, Rootin' Tootin' Raspberry, Choo-Choo Cherry

15. Darrin Stephens, Becky Conner, Gordon on *Sesame Street*

16. Jell-O Pudding, Kodak, Coca-Cola

17. "The Monsters Are Due On Maple Street," "Time Enough at Last," "Long Distance Call"

18. Leonard McCoy, Beverly Crusher, Julian Bashir

19. "Mind Games," "What Is Life," "It Don't Come Easy"

20. Captain Crook, Hamburglar, The Grimace

THE NEGLECTED LETTERS

Described below are pop culture items that begin with the letters Q, X, or Z. Identify them all.

1. '70s PBS kids show from Boston, Mass.
2. Cereal with a Martian mascot
3. Star of *Destiny Turns on the Radio*
4. Better known as the Happy Hooker
5. "She's Not There" and "Tell Her No" were their big hits.
6. The Who album and movie
7. Jack Klugman played a medical examiner on this show.
8. Olivia Newton-John movie
9. TV show in which Scott Bakula inhabited different bodies through time
10. Sang "Senses Working Overtime" and "Dear God"
11. Scully and Mulder's particular interest
12. Ad slogan: "You're not fully clean unless you're ___ fully clean"
13. Sang "Radio Ga Ga" and "Bohemian Rhapsody"
14. Brazilian children's TV show host
15. Bandleader who married Charo
16. George Hamilton spoof about a swishy swashbuckler
17. 1994 flick about the *Twenty-One* scandal
18. Long-bearded rockers who spin their guitars around
19. Ray Milland–Roger Corman film
20. Chocolate or strawberry milk additive

Hawaiian Luau of Puzzlers

In celebration of our glorious fiftieth state, answer these pop culture trivia questions about Hawaii. Then enjoy a heaping bowl of poi.

1. Name the signature song of entertainer Don Ho.
2. Donny and Marie were pursued by bumbling jewel thieves in what movie set in Hawaii?
3. Give the full name of Tom Selleck's character on *Magnum, P.I.*
4. In what movie did Elvis sing, "Rock-A-Hula Baby" and "I Can't Help Falling in Love with You"?
5. Name the game show hosted by Bob Eubanks in which contestants had to grab flying dollar bills while enclosed in a glass booth.
6. Who was Steve McGarrett's arch enemy?
7. According to the commercial, how many kinds of fruit are in Hawaiian Punch?
8. In *The Brady Bunch* Hawaiian episodes, Bobby found a tiki idol that placed a curse on members of the Brady clan. What curses befell Peter, Greg, and Alice respectively?
9. Who sang the theme song for the 1981 *Love Boat* clone, *Aloha Paradise*?
10. Appearing on network TV mere days before *Miami Vice*, this Hawaiian cop show only lasted three months.
11. Name the series that starred Anthony Eisley and Robert Conrad as Hawaiian cops.
   BONUS: In *Ma and Pa Kettle at Waikiki*, how did Pa inadvertently increase productivity at a pineapple factory?

DAY IN, DAY OUT

Listed below are twenty-five pop culture items with the days of the week in their names. Name them all.

1. The Mamas and the Papas song
2. Lead character in *Dragnet*
3. Bay City Rollers song
4. Jodie Foster movie
5. Spanky and Our Gang song (two possible answers)
6. Movie featuring Donna Summer's hit "Last Dance"
7. Easybeats song
8. *Addams Family* character
9. Rolling Stones song
10. Movie series with hockey-mask-wearing villain
11. Fleetwood Mac song
12. Movie about whirlwind tour of Europe

13. Song by Chicago
14. Sang "Voices Carry"
15. Song by The Cure
16. Jane Fonda movie
17. Morphine song in *Spanking the Monkey*
18. Melanie Griffith–Sting movie
19. Bangles song written by Prince
20. John Travolta movie
21. U2 song
22. Walter Matthau–Jill Clayburgh movie
23. Morrissey song
24. Movie directed by Billy Crystal
25. Played Thalia Menninger on *Dobie Gillis*

INITIAL RESPONSE

All the celebrities described below have double initials (i.e., R. R., B. B., etc.) If you can name them all, well, that's pretty good, I guess.

1. Former husband of Julia Roberts
2. Bit the head off a bat on stage
3. TV's Buck Rogers
4. Charlie Sheen's brother
5. Left *CBS Evening News* in 1995
6. Played Ethel Mertz
7. Founded Sundance Film Institute
8. Won 1993 Oscar for playing a mute
9. Played a dumb American in *A Fish Called Wanda*
10. Founded *Playboy* magazine
11. Brad from *The Rocky Horror Picture Show*
12. One of two Marilyns on *The Munsters*
13. CNN and TBS magnate
14. David on *Eight Is Enough*
15. Sang "Montego Bay"
16. Frequent star of Broadway's *Hello, Dolly!*
17. Author of *Fried Green Tomatoes at the Whistle Stop Cafe* and a frequent *Match Game* celebrity
18. Her last film was *The Misfits*

19. Had roles on *Diff'rent Strokes*, *Good Times*, and *Fame*, and once sang "Who's that eating that nasty food?"
20. Rock Hudson's co-star in *Pillow Talk*
21. Director of *The Sugarland Express* and *Duel*
22. Star of *Thelma and Louise*
23. Sang theme to *Mad Max: Beyond Thunderdome*
24. Director of *The Four Seasons*
25. Narrated the original *Untouchables* TV show
26. Uhura on *Star Trek*
27. Former U.S. president/B-movie star
28. *The Executioner's Song* is about him
29. Elly May on *The Beverly Hillbillies*
30. Marcia Brady on *The Brady Bunch*
31. Female lead in *Die Hard* and *Die Hard II*
32. Star of *Oh, Heavenly Dog!*

ANSWERS

1. Lyle Lovett
2. Ozzy Osbourne
3. Gil Girard
4. Emilio Estevez
5. Connie Chung
6. Vivian Vance
7. Robert Redford
8. Holly Hunter
9. Kevin Kline
10. Hugh Hefner
11. Barry Bostwick
12. Pat Priest
13. Ted Turner
14. Grant Goodeve
15. Bobby Bloom
16. Carol Channing
17. Fannie Flagg
18. Marilyn Monroe
19. Janet Jackson
20. Doris Day
21. Steven Spielberg
22. Susan Sarandon
23. Tina Turner
24. Alan Alda
25. Walter Winchell
26. Nichelle Nichols
27. Ronald Reagan
28. Gary Gilmore
29. Donna Douglas
30. Maureen McCormick
31. Bonnie Bedelia
32. Chevy Chase

Acronymous

What do these pop culture acronyms stand for? If you can identify ten or more, treat yourself to a **B.L.T.**

1. *M*A*S*H
2. R.E.M.
3. *CHiPs*
4. The U.N.C.L.E. in *The Man from U.N.C.L.E.*
5. *C.H.O.M.P.S.*
6. The R.F.D. in *Mayberry R.F.D.*
7. *C.H.U.D.*
8. The RC in RC Cola
9. *M.A.S.K.*
10. OMD
11. *S.W.A.T.*
12. *M.A.N.T.I.S.*
13. A & P
14. ELO
15. B.A.D.
16. The E.A.R.T.H. in *E.A.R.T.H. Force*

LET'S BE FRANK

Described below are famous Franks, both real and fictitious. Identify them all, but don't call them Francis.

1. Ol' Blue Eyes
2. Annette Funicello's *Beach Party* co-star
3. Character on *Murphy Brown*
4. Villain in *Blue Velvet*
5. The Sweet Transvestite from Transsexual, Transylvania
6. Singer of the theme from the movie *Grease*
7. His albums include *Uncle Meat* and *Lumpy Gravy*
8. *ABC World News Tonight* anchor from 1978 to 1983
9. Laverne's dad
10. Director of *It's a Wonderful Life*
11. Sang "Sea Cruise"
12. Star of 1979's *Dracula*
13. Host of *Monday Night Football*; married to Kathie Lee
14. Penned *Batman: The Dark Knight Returns*
15. Voice of Miss Piggy and Fozzie Bear
16. Had ongoing affair with "Hotlips" Houlihan
17. Played the Riddler on TV's *Batman*
18. Benji's trainer
19. Sgt. Carter on TV's *Gomer Pyle, USMC*
20. Played the title character in *The Wizard of Oz*

And I did it My Way ...

ANSWERS

1. Frank Sinatra
2. Frankie Avalon
3. Frank Fontana
4. Frank Booth
5. Frank N. Furter
6. Frankie Valli
7. Frank Zappa
8. Frank Reynolds
9. Frank DeFazio
10. Frank Capra
11. Frankie Ford
12. Frank Langella
13. Frank Gifford
14. Frank Miller
15. Frank Oz
16. Frank Burns
17. Frank Gorshin
18. Frank Inn
19. Frank Sutton
20. Frank Morgan

BOTANICAL BAFFLERS

The pop culture items described below contain plants in their names. Identify them all correctly and someday you too may harness the sun's light for nourishment.

1. Tiny Tim's claim to fame
2. Overblown Oliver Stone mini-series
3. Movie loosely based on the life of Janis Joplin
4. Sang "Running Up That Hill"
5. The Freddy Krueger saga
6. Thinly veiled Coasters' song about VD
7. Where Natalie Wood and Warren Beatty play young lovers
8. Waif-like Calvin Klein supermodel
9. Marvin Gaye hit co-opted by the California Raisins
10. Wife of Herman Munster
11. Nick Nolte playwright-in-prison movie
12. Sister of Bo and Luke
13. Powdered milk brand
14. WKRP nighttime DJ
15. What Fred Flintstone's lodge buddies drink
16. Star of *Moonstruck* and *Little Shop of Horrors*
17. Val Kilmer swashbuckler
18. Sang "Ah, Leah" and "Do You Compute?"
19. Porky Pig's girlfriend
20. Their biggest hit was "Elvira"

Hey! I demand royalties for this quiz!

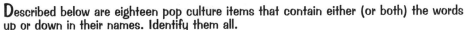

Ups and Downs

Described below are eighteen pop culture items that contain either (or both) the words <u>up</u> or <u>down</u> in their names. Identify them all.

_____ 1. Men at Work song that mentions a Vegemite sandwich

_____ 2. Tim Matheson raft racing movie

_____ 3. Novel by Richard Adams about a society of intelligent rabbits

_____ 4. Host of *20/20*

_____ 5. The Uncola

_____ 6. Hit song from The Rolling Stones' *Tattoo You* album

_____ 7. Sandy Dennis played a NYC high school teacher in this movie

_____ 8. Billy Joel's love note to Christie Brinkley

_____ 9. American remake of *Boudu Saved from Drowning*

_____ 10. Diana Ross disco tune

_____ 11. Petula Clark's ode to the big city

_____ 12. According to the Drifters, the place to be when "this whole world starts getting you down"

_____ 13. *Animal House*-type movie made by *Mad* magazine

_____ 14. Line that follows "Do a little dance, make a little love"

_____ 15. Fifth Dimension song

_____ 16. Movie in which Charlton Heston was the captain of a nuclear submarine

_____ 17. Sylvester Stallone prison flick

_____ 18. Richard Pryor played three roles in this film

Spin Again, or Lose a Turn

Following are the descriptions of twenty games. Name the games—and win!

1. Put hotels on large portions of Atlantic City.

2. Remove plastic organs with tweezers.

3. Fit geometric shapes into holes before "plunger" pops up.

4. Roll dice and assemble an insect.

5. Satiate water cows craving for marbles.

6. Make way through confectionery landmarks.

7. Get a job, have kids, and drive a car.

8. Gyrate on a mat with colored dots, but don't fall down.

9. Shout out a letter and a number and hope for a Hit, not a Miss.

10. Press levers to get all your balls on your opponent's side.

11. Keep the kid from falling into the frozen pond.

12. It's like Tiddly Winks with insects and trousers.

13. Hook together a long string of simians.

14. Do good things and climb up, do bad things and slide down.

15. Basis for bad movie with multiple endings.

16. Open the door and hope you don't end up with a geek.

17. Flip small plastic disks into giant rotating orifice.

18. Build a Rube-Goldbergesque contraption to catch a rodent.

19. Throw beanbags at Tic-Tac-Toe board.

20. Land on another person's piece to send them back home, then maniacally press the Pop-O-Matic bubble.

ANSWERS

1. Monopoly
2. Operation
3. Perfection
4. Cootie
5. Hungry Hungry Hippos
6. Candy Land
7. (The Game of) Life
8. Twister
9. Battleship
10. Gnip Gnop
11. Don't Break the Ice
12. Ants in the Pants
13. Barrel of Monkeys
14. Chutes and Ladders
15. Clue
16. Mystery Date
17. Mr. Mouth
18. Mousetrap
19. Toss Across
20. Trouble

CANDY IS DANDY

Name the candy for which these advertising slogans were created.

1. Melts in your mouth, not in your hands
2. Sometimes you feel like a nut…
3. …sometimes you don't.
4. The Great American Chocolate Bar
5. Two great tastes that taste great together
6. You can roll it to your pal
7. Taste a rainbow of fruit flavors
8. Chocolate is scrunch-ous when it crunches
9. No matter how you slice it, it comes up peanuts
10. Whatever it is I think I see becomes this
11. Makes mouths happy
12. A burst of refreshing fruit flavor—*for you!*
13. He didn't know the gum was loaded

14. One today helps you work, rest, and play
15. A "touch" of fudge
16. Get the Sensation
17. The chocolate-covered caramel with the cookie crunch
18. Lasts a good long time
19. First it's a candy, then it's a gum
20. The gum that won't stick to your face
21. It's too good for kids; it's made for grown-ups
22. Charlie says, "Gee, it's really swell"
23. I was right in the middle of one when I found gold
24. The Freshmaker
25. A part of living

Coin-Op Videogame Jamboree

Part 1: Identify these video games from the early '80s.

1. Orange bi-ped with trunk jumps around on a pyramid
2. Insane man scales building and evades dropped flowerpots
3. Yellow circle devours dots and runs from multicolored ghosts
4. Squat Italian tries to rescue damsel from barrel-throwing ape
5. Energetic amphibian attempts to safely cross street
6. Diamond-shaped thing shoots at advancing multi-legged arthropod
7. Pookas and Fygars chase you underground
8. Space jet strafes elaborate floating space platform

Part 2:

Match the character descriptions with the games (listed below) in which they appeared.

1. Flying ostriches
2. Gun-toting archeologist
3. Mouse in security guard uniform
4. Clown with ball
5. Pig with bows and arrows in a hot air balloon
6. Light cycles
7. A walking fried egg
8. Bear with a wizard's cap

A. *Mappy*
B. *Pooyan*
C. *Burger Time*
D. *Joust*
E. *Tutenkam*
F. *Crystal Castles*
G. *Mr. Do*
H. *Tron*

ANSWERS

Part 1:
1. Q*Bert
2. Crazy Climber
3. Pac Man
4. Donkey Kong
5. Frogger
6. Centipede (or Millipede)
7. Dig Dug
8. Zaxxon

Part 2:
1. D
2. E
3. A
4. G
5. B
6. H
7. C
8. F

AD IT UP

Name the products or companies for which these ad slogans were written.

1. You deserve a break today.
2. It's the real thing.
3. Mmmm mmmm good!
4. The king of beers
5. Proud as a peacock
6. The cheese that goes crunch
7. The heartbeat of America
8. The quicker picker-upper
9. Good to the last drop
10. Strong enough for a man, but made for a woman
11. You're in good hands.
12. Fly the friendly skies.
13. Let your fingers do the walking.
14. Get a piece of the rock.
15. If you've got the time, we've got the beer.
16. Three temperatures—one detergent
17. The best part of waking up
18. Quality is job one.
19. Have it your way.
20. They make money the old fashioned way—they earn it.
21. For bouncin' and behavin' hair
22. The best a man can get
23. It takes a licking and keeps on ticking.
24. Plop plop fizz fizz
25. The choice of a new generation
26. Pure brewed in God's country
27. The dogs kids love to bite
28. Gets the red out
29. Tastes good like a cigarette should
30. Ring-around-the-collar

TRUE COLORS

Each of the thirty things described below has a color mentioned in its names. Can you name them all?

1. Captain Kangaroo's rural buddy
2. Album and movie by Prince
3. Kids' shoe mascot
4. '70s high-school basketball drama
5. Diamond in first Inspector Clouseau movie
6. Ultra-violent Stanley Kubrick epic
7. The place for the seafood lover in you
8. Curious George's keeper
9. 1966 Los Bravos hit
10. First Gene Wilder–Richard Pryor film
11. Popeye's girlfriend
12. *Rocky Horror Picture Show* maid
13. Recorded "White Room"
14. Former *Golden Girl* and host of game show *Just Men!*
15. Destination of Dorothy and Toto
16. Roald Dahl book about a fruit-riding youngster
17. Slushy fast-food beverage found in malls
18. '80s pop-music countdown show with dancers
19. Otherworldly mammalian visitor to the Neighborhood of Make-Believe
20. "Everything's better" with this on it
21. Town flirt in *It's a Wonderful Life*
22. Robert Conrad WWII series
23. Erotic anthology show on Showtime
24. Movie in which a nuclear-armed blimp disrupts the Super Bowl
25. Tommy James and the Shondells hit remade by Joan Jett
26. Multicultural '70s kids show
27. Pumpkin-throwing nemesis to Spiderman
28. Pirate movie satire from 1983
29. Female folk duo
30. Cartoon studio in *Who Framed Roger Rabbit?*

ANSWERS

1. Mr. Green Jeans
2. *Purple Rain*
3. Buster Brown
4. *The White Shadow*
5. The Pink Panther
6. *A Clockwork Orange*
7. Red Lobster
8. The Man in the Yellow Hat
9. "Black Is Black"
10. *Silver Streak*
11. Olive Oyl
12. Magenta
13. Cream
14. Betty White
15. The Emerald City
16. *James and the Giant Peach*
17. Orange Julius
18. *Solid Gold*
19. The Purple Panda
20. Blue Bonnet margarine
21. Violet Bick
22. *Baa Baa Black Sheep*
23. *Red Shoe Diaries*
24. *Black Sunday*
25. "Crimson and Clover"
26. *Big Blue Marble*
27. The Green Goblin
28. *Yellowbeard*
29. Indigo Girls
30. Maroon Cartoons

See You in the Funny Papers

In which comic strips, both past and present, might you find these scenarios?

1. A beagle pretends to gun down the Red Baron.
2. The General ogles his secretary.
3. A fat cat eats lasagna.
4. An office worker is taunted by his dog and upper management.
5. The principal characters refer to each other as "pet."
6. "The Spook" tries to escape from prison.
7. Dan Quayle is represented by a feather, and a talking cigarette encourages smoking.
8. The youngest boy in the family has a pet iguana named Quincy.
9. A harried working woman deals with her husband and daughter.
10. A harried working woman eats too much chocolate.
11. A hapless Viking gets yelled at by his wife.
12. A young girl hangs out with a ruffian named Sluggo.
13. The husband makes a really big sandwich, and sleeps on the couch.
14. A boy and his tiger go sledding with wild abandon.
15. A newspaper editing bird gets lunch at Roz's Diner.
16. A large, angry cavewoman clubs a snake to a pulp.
17. Children blame invisible people Not Me and Ida Know for their misdeeds.
18. A mischieveous young boy annoys Mr. Wilson.
19. A penguin looks for his mother and an ugly cat runs for president.
20. A baby talks to sunbeams, and neighbor Thirsty likes to drink.

CATCH THE PHRASE

Part 1: Listed below are catch phrases that permeated our vernacular at some time or another. Identify the character who first uttered them, then never utter them again. Please.

1. "Kiss my grits."
2. "Go ahead. Make my day."
3. "Don't have a cow, man."
4. "Yabba Dabba Doo!"
5. "To the moon, Alice!"
6. "Shazbat!"
7. "Ayyyyyyyyyyyyy!"
8. "Up your nose with a rubber hose."
9. "Book 'em, Dano."
10. "Make it so."
11. "Dynomite!"
12. "Take off, hoser."
13. "No problem."
14. "Veddy interesting."
15. "Who loves ya, baby?"
16. "Hey, hey, hey."
17. "Whatchoo talkin' 'bout?"
18. "Just the facts, ma'am."
19. "Good grief!"
20. "De-plane. De-plane."
21. "Stifle yourself."
    HIPSTER BONUS: "Shut yer stinkin' trap."

Part 2: Here's a special section for fans of <u>Saturday Night Live</u>. Name the characters that uttered these saucy bon mots.

1. "We're gonna *pump* you up."
2. "We are two wild and crazy guys."
3. "O-tay!"
4. "Isn't that special?"
5. "Never mind."
6. "Base-a-ball been berry berry good to me."
7. "You look mah-vah-lous."
8. "Schwiiiing!"
9. "Consume mass quantities."
10. "It just goes to show you . . . it's always something."
11. "Jane, you ignorant slut."
12. "Oh no!"
13. "We have diverticulitis."
14. "But nooooooo."

ANSWERS

Part 1:
1. Flo Castleberry (from *Alice*)
2. Dirty Harry (*Sudden Impact*)
3. Bart Simpson
4. Fred Flintstone
5. Ralph Kramden
6. Mork from Ork
7. The Fonz
8. Vinnie Barbarino
9. Steve McGarrett
10. Capt. Jean-Luc Picard
11. J.J. Evans (from *Good Times*)
12. Bob and Doug McKenzie
13. ALF
14. Arte Johnson's German guy on *Laugh-In*
15. Kojak
16. Fat Albert
17. Arnold Jackson (from *Diff'rent Strokes*)
18. Sgt. Joe Friday
19. Charlie Brown
20. Tattoo
21. Archie Bunker
HIPSTER BONUS: Skank on *The Ben Stiller Show*

Part 2:
1. Hans and Franz
2. The Czech (or Festrunk) Brothers
3. Buckwheat
4. The Church Lady
5. Emily Litella
6. Chico Escuela
7. Fernando
8. Wayne and Garth
9. The Coneheads
10. Rosanne Rosannadanna
11. Dan Aykroyd on *Weekend Update*
12. Mr. Bill
13. Doug and Wendy Whiner
14. John Belushi on *Weekend Update*

MANY TOYS FOR BOYS AND GIRLS

 Identify the twenty-five toys described below.

1. Multi-colored pegs inserted in an illuminated board
2. They wobble, but they don't fall down.
3. Anthropomorphic tuber with removable features
4. Loosely coiled spring that walks down stairs
5. Play-Doh dental excavation kit
6. Brown wooden building materials named after a president
7. Drawing board with dials, for the ultra-coordinated
8. Danish multi-hued bricks with raised dots for easy snap-together assembly
9. Boxing ring with sparring mechanical men
10. Famous war hero doll with three-day beard
11. Bounceable, malleable compound used to duplicate images from the funnies
12. Grossly proportioned dream girl
13. Stereoscope viewer with delightful film wheels
14. Long-haired pastel horses
15. Super-elastic muscleman
16. Decorated plastic do-hickeys that get smaller when you cook them
17. Green goop with snot-like consistency
18. Large rotating disk for seated floor-spinning action
19. Series of plastic gears used to make cool designs
20. Giant inflatable ball for children to straddle and bounce on
21. Plastic tricyle with oversized front wheel
22. Canine pull-toy with detective cap
23. Record-playing train engine
24. Trash-eating farm animal
25. Bald puppet with many disguises

Department of Transportation

Described below are famous modes of transportation from TV, movies, and music. Identify them all.

1. Ship captained by Merrill Stubing
2. Psychedelic Beatles' vehicle in movie and song
3. Name for Bo and Luke Duke's 1969 Dodge Charger
4. Speed Racer's hi-tech race car
5. Mr. Rogers' transport to the Neighborhood of Make Believe
6. Gilligan and the Skipper led three-hour tours on this
7. Pontiac Trans Am driven by Michael Knight
8. Magical flying jalopy in Dick Van Dyke movie
9. Herbie the Volkswagen's nickname
10. Spaceship piloted by Han Solo
11. Mobile van driven by Scooby Doo's gang
12. Code name for squad car driven by Malloy and Reed
13. Train engine in *Dumbo*
14. Roving landcraft used in Saturday morning show set in the twenty-fifth century
15. Craft Carl Sagan used to explore the cosmos
16. What Gladys Knight had "a one-way ticket back" on
17. Spacecraft flown by Super Marionette Colonel Steve Zodiac
18. Wreck of yore remembered by Gordon Lightfoot
19. Wretched sitcom starring Jerry Van Dyke and and a matronly talking vehicle
20. Wonderbug's alter ego

PETS AND THEIR PEOPLE

Match the famous pets on the left with their famous owners on the right, then state what kind of animal each pet is. And remember to have your pet spayed or neutered.

_____ 1. Bandit
_____ 2. Dollar
_____ 3. Abraham
_____ 4. Bear
_____ 5. Dino
_____ 6. Ruff
_____ 7. Tweety
_____ 8. Tramp
_____ 9. Mr. Ed
_____ 10. Chim Chim
_____ 11. Hot Dog
_____ 12. Flipper
_____ 13. Ben
_____ 14. Spot
_____ 15. Eddie
_____ 16. Duke
_____ 17. Shep
_____ 18. Kvaak
_____ 19. Opus
_____ 20. Sebastian

A. Martin Crane
B. Alexandra Cabot
C. Granny
D. Dennis the Menace
E. Binkley
F. Wilbur Post
G. George of the Jungle
H. Hagar the Horrible
I. Arnold Jackson
J. The Munsters
K. Richie Rich
L. Jonny Quest
M. B.J.
N. The Douglases
O. The Clampetts
P. Spridal Racer
Q. Fred Flintstone
R. Jughead Jones
S. Sandy and Bud Ricks
T. "Grizzly" Adams

KEN BERRY VS. BILL BIXBY

Ken Berry and Bill Bixby were all over television and the movies in the '60s, '70s, and '80s. Your job is to attribute either Berry or Bixby to each one of the projects listed below.

1. *The Cat from Outer Space*
2. *My Favorite Martian*
3. *The Incredible Hulk*
4. *Once upon a Mattress*
5. *Mama's Family*
6. *F-Troop*
7. *Clambake*
8. *Mayberry RFD*
9. *Blossom*
10. *The Courtship of Eddie's Father*
11. *Hello Down There*
12. *Rich Man, Poor Man*
13. *Private Secretary*
14. *The Apple Dumpling Gang*
15. *Herbie Rides Again*
16. Kinney Shoes ads
17. *The Ann Sothern Show*
18. *Goodnight Beantown*
19. *The Magician*
20. *Kentucky Fried Movie*

One of These Things Is Not Like the Other

In each group, figure out which item does not belong, and state the common ground of the three remaining things. There's probably more than one right answer for some of these, but you must pick the one I've picked to get any points. So there.

1. wheelbarrow
   anvil
   thimble
   race car

2. *Play It Again, Sam*
   The Front
   Sleeper
   Scenes from a Mall

3. Cookie Monster
   Big Bird
   Fozzie Bear
   Oscar the Grouch

4. The Incredible Hulk
   The Sub-Mariner
   Superman
   The Punisher

5. Kit Kat
   Almond Joy
   Reese's Peanut
     Butter Cups
   Twix

6. *Singled Out*
   The Love Connection
   The Newlywed Game
   The Dating Game

7. Sonny and Cher
   Shields and Yarnell
   Donny and Marie
   Burns and Allen

8. Marvin Gaye
   Otis Redding
   Buddy Holly
   Ricky Nelson

9. *The Graduate*
   Rain Man
   Tootsie
   Midnight Cowboy

10. *The Fly*
    The Blob
    *Invasion of the Body
      Snatchers*
    Freaks

11. Charlie Watts
    Ringo Starr
    Keith Moon
    Jeff Beck

12. Hawaii
    Mount Rushmore
    The Grand Canyon
    King's Island, OH

13. Nero Wolfe
    Ellery Queen
    Frank Cannon
    "The Fatman"

14. "Goodbye Girl"
    "Last Kiss"
    "Tell Laura I Love
      Her"
    "Leader of the Pack"

15. Bumble Bee
    Mr. Clean
    Chicken of the Sea
    Starkist

16. *The Boatniks*
    That Darn Cat
    The Aristocats
    Candleshoe

1. anvil; Monopoly game pieces
2. *Sleeper*; movies starring, but not directed by, Woody Allen
3. Fozzie Bear; Muppets introduced on *Sesame Street*
4. Superman; Marvel Comics
5. Kit Kat; candy bars packaged in two pieces
6. *The Newlywed Game*; game shows that match up single folks
7. Donny and Marie; married entertainers
8. Marvin Gaye; rock stars
9. *Rain Man*: Films for which Dustin Hoffman was nominated for a Best Actor Oscar, but didn't win
10. *Freaks*; horror movies that have been re-made
11. Jeff Beck; rock drummers
12. Mount Rushmore; places who died in plane crashes
13. Ellery Queen; characters played by William Conrad
14. "Goodbye Girl"; songs about teenage death
15. Mr. Clean; brands of tuna
16. *The Aristocats*; Live-action Disney movies

MAGAZINE MANIA

Name the magazines that do the following:

1. Picks the "50 Most Beautiful People in the World"

2. Condenses novels and provides opportunities to "Enrich Your Word Power"

3. Compares photos of two different celebrities, humorously positing that they have been "Separated at Birth"

4. Dubs someone "Man of the Year"

5. Includes a gatefold photo of a naked lady in the middle, with "Party Jokes" on the back

6. Reviews new music, and co-funded the movie *Perfect*

7. Prints cerebral cartoons and weekly events happening in the Big Apple

8. Delights male sports fans and angers church groups with their yearly "Swimsuit Issue"

9. Does wacky parodies of movies and TV, and chronicles the adversarial relationship between a white and black spy

10. Gives certain products their self-named "Seal of Approval"

11. Makes a list of 500 companies with highest gross revenue

12. Details the adventures of "Goofus and Gallant"

13. Puts hotshot computer execs on their fluorescent colored covers, then updates their "Hot" on-line version

14. Doles out a weekly list of "Cheers & Jeers" concerning the world of television

15. Shocks the world with nude Demi Moore covers

16. Prints "Index" of interesting numerical facts

17. Reviews movies, TV, books, multimedia, and videos with letter grades every week.

REPTILES AND AMPHIBIANS

Each of the fifteen pop-culture references described below contains a type of reptile or amphibian. Identify them all, then shed your skin.

1. Hit for Culture Club
2. Car care product / consolation prize on game shows
3. Nickname of child in *Aliens*
4. Repulsive Monty Python candy
5. Paul Hogan's outback hero
6. *Wind in the Willows* hero
7. His quest is to leave the zoo and return to the Everglades.
8. Movie in which Richard Burton plays a drunk clergyman
9. According to Three Dog Night, what Jeremiah was
10. 1976 Burt Reynolds sequel to *White Lightning*
11. Cartoon hero whose sidekick is Dum Dum
12. Michael Douglas's character in *Wall Street*
13. Nickname for Jim Morrison
14. Gravelly voiced Our Gang member
15. Main protagonist of *Escape from New York* and *Escape from L.A.*

Cereals Fortified with Fun

Name the cereal mascots described below, then name their respective cereals.

1. Muscular bipedal jungle cat
2. Insane bird
3. Baseball cap wearing son of Question #1
4. Onomatopoeic elves
5. Pathetic, ever-pleading hare
6. Baked-good-thieving dog
7. Hand-slapping, husky-voiced frog
8. Grandfatherly ship's officer
9. Martian with propellor sprouting from head
10. Lumberjack nemesis of #9

11. Multi-colored long-beaked jungle bird
12. Spectacled brown miniature pachyderm
13. Evasive leprechaun
14. Cuddly porcupine
15. Smooth-talking bear
16. Everpresent nectar-toting insect
17. Blue ghost that sounds like Peter Lorre
BONUS FUN: In addition to #17, name the other four cereals in the series based on famous monsters

ANSWERS

1. Tony the Tiger, Kellogg's Frosted Flakes
2. Sonny Cuckoo, General Mills' Cocoa Puffs
3. Tony Jr., Kellogg's Frosted Rice
4. Snap, Crackle and Pop; Kellogg's Rice Krispies
5. The Rabbit (or Silly Rabbit), General Mills' Trix
6. Chip the Cookie Hound, General Mills' Cookie Crisp
7. Dig 'Em, Kellogg's Sugar Smacks
8. Cap'n Crunch, Quaker's Cap'n Crunch
9. Quisp, Quaker's Quisp
10. Quake, Quaker's Quake
11. Toucan Sam, Kellogg's Froot Loops
12. Tusk-Tusk, Kellogg's Cocoa Krispies
13. Lucky, General Mills' Lucky Charms
14. Poppy, Kellogg's Sugar Corn Pops
15. Sugar Bear, Post Super Sugar Crisp
16. Honey Nut Bee, General Mills' Honey Nut Cheerios
17. Boo Berry; General Mills' Boo Berry
BONUS: Count Chocula, Franken Berry, Fruit Brute, Yummy Mummy (all by General Mills)

PITCHIN' WHO?

Described below are twenty advertising creations. Identify these product trademark characters and the products they pitched to learn the ancient Chinese secret.

1. Toilet-paper-obsessed grocery store manager
2. Snack-cake-shaped cowboy
3. Finicky orange cat
4. Detergent-soaking beautician
5. Suicidal cartoon tuna with good taste
6. Mountain-grown-coffee hawker
7. Quicker picker-upper waitress
8. Antacid-shaped boy
9. Violent fruit drink pitchboy
10. Ate cereal, even though he hates everything
11. Cheese-snack-lovin' jungle cat
12. Beer-swilling frat dog
13. Gargantuan plant-man hybrid
14. Red-bearded conjuring fast food monarch
15. Commode-dwelling sailor
16. Pink bass-drum-playing hare
17. Top-hat bedecked *Arachis hypogaea* seed pod
18. A pink man made of bubble-bath soap
19. Red-headed clown in a yellow suit and big floppy shoes
20. Giggly chef-hat-wearing pastry boy whose tummy is ripe for pokin'

ALIAS SMITH AND JONES

The twenty-two people described below all have either the last name of Smith or Jones. Name them all!

1. Partridge Family matriarch
2. Hightower in the *Police Academy* movies
3. A.k.a. The Fresh Prince
4. Voice of Darth Vader
5. Left The Clash to form Big Audio Dynamite
6. Only actress to stay during full run of *Charlie's Angels*
7. Creator of the Road Runner and Wile E. Coyote
8. The cute Monkee
9. Sweaty singer of "What's New, Pussycat?"
10. Director of *Erik the Viking*
11. Rolling Stone who drowned in 1969
12. Allison on *Melrose Place*
13. Ran with the wolves in *Never Cry Wolf*
14. Wooed Valerie Bertinelli in the TV movie *Sooner or Later*
15. Played title role in *Vamp*
16. TV's Morticia Addams
17. Star of *The Million Dollar Duck*
18. Recorded classic album *Horses*
19. Voice of Lisa Simpson
20. Sang "Chuck E.'s In Love"
21. Howdy Doody's human friend
22. Has played Ty Cobb and Loretta Lynn's hubby

Flesh for Fantasy

Described below are fourteen pop culture items which feature the word <u>meat</u>, a type of meat or meat product. Name them all.

1. Shari Lewis's sock friend
2. David Naughton movie about a wacky band of downhill skiers
3. Sang "Two Out of Three Ain't Bad"
4. Stuttered "That's All Folks"
5. Got a small town to dance again in *Footloose*
6. Dean Martin hosted many of these star-studded gag fests
7. Mike Stivic's nickname
8. Clara Peller's infamous TV ad utterance
9. Movie in which Don Knotts spent a night in a haunted house
10. Title of Bobcat Goldthwait album
11. Plays King Kaiser in *My Favorite Year*
12. Sam I Am pushes these
13. Dick Van Dyke movie about a town that quits smoking
14. Was defeated by Perry Mason almost every week

ANSWERS

1. Lamb Chop
2. *Hot Dog . . . The Movie*
3. Meat Loaf
4. Porky Pig
5. Kevin Bacon
6. Celebrity roast
7. Meathead
8. "Where's the beef?"
9. *The Ghost and Mr. Chicken*
10. *Meat Bob*
11. Joseph Bologna
12. Green eggs and ham
13. *Cold Turkey*
14. Hamilton Burger

THE MAGICAL POP CULTURE WORD CHAIN

Each of the following clues can be solved with a two-word answer. Each successive answer contains one word from the previous answer. No word is featured in more than two answers in a row. The answer to Clue #21 refers back to the answer to Clue #1, thus creating an exciting chain of pop culture. Complete this chain, then consider yourself a Cultural Idiot.

1. Frontman for The News
2. Spastic funnyman beloved in France
3. Ben and Jerry named an ice cream flavor after him
4. Star of *When a Man Loves a Woman* and *Hero*
5. Walter Lantz cartoon creation
6. Violet-colored visitor to the Neighborhood of Make Believe
7. Sang "Smoke on the Water"
8. Laurence Fishburne/Jeff Goldblum film
9. Make-up by Noxema
10. Elvis flick set in Ft. Lauderdale
11. Early hit by The Who
12. Ex-Green Beret protector-of-hippies played by Tom Laughlin
13. Beverage named after President Carter's brother
14. Game played by Bob and Doug MacKenzie on their album
15. Wrote "Fear and Loathing in Las Vegas"
16. Sang "Hold Me Now"
17. Teenage Super Friends
18. Flies an invisible plane
19. Film in which Julia Roberts plays a prostitute
20. Film in which Brooke Shields plays a prostitute
21. Giant infantile cartoon duck

SHTICK TO IT!

If you performed the following behaviors, which comedians would you be? Name them all to avoid heckling from the back row.

1. Wear a fake arrow through your head.
2. Smash watermelons with a sledgehammer.
3. Utter seven words you can't say on television.
4. Complain about not getting respect.
5. Sit in a giant rocking chair.
6. Inflate a rubber glove with your nose.
7. Tell stories about your drug-related accident.
8. Recite obscene nursery rhymes.
9. Deliver surreal one-liners in a monotone.
10. Do an impression of Elmer Fudd singing Bruce Springsteen's "Fire."
11. Scream, wear a beret, and complain about women.
12. Declare yourself a "domestic goddess."
13. Play an accordion in a tacky dress.
14. Tell stories about fatherhood.
15. Deliver acute observations while sporting a Prince Valiant haircut.
16. Read the precedings of your obscenity trial onstage.
17. Do a mock interview as a 2000-year-old man.
18. Confide in your audience with a terse, "Can we talk?"
19. Read "The Great Gatsby" aloud from cover to cover until you're booed off the stage.
20. Do a sitcom about "nothing."

Bursting with Fruit Flavors

The following pop culture items all contain a type of fruit in their names. Name them all, then reward yourself with a refreshing kumquat.

1. Prince song about a hat
2. Legendary Harlem Globetrotter
3. Giant purple cartoon primate
4. Elusive evil character in *The Third Man*
5. Disco duet that sang "Shake Your Groove Thing"
6. Low-budget Melanie Griffith action film
7. Record label started by the Beatles
8. Composed ethereal music for *Risky Business* and *Miracle Mile*
9. Richie Cunningham sang this to indicate he was horny
10. Bingo, Fleegle, Drooper, and Snorky
11. Malcolm McDowell drank drugged milk in this flick
12. Psychedelic band responsible for "Incense and Peppermints"
13. Fictional town where the SCTV studios are located
14. Academic murder suspect in the game of Clue

AUNTS AND UNCLES

Described below are a dozen famous aunts and uncles from the realm of pop culture. Identify them all.

1. Dorothy saw her face in the Witch's crystal ball.
2. Cooked and cleaned for Mike, Robbie, and Chip
3. Sparred with Fred Sanford
4. Penny-pinching kin of Donald Duck
5. Absent-minded babysitter for Tabitha Stevens
6. Her face adorns boxes of pancake mix.
7. Made delicious pies for Opie
8. Depending on the source, either Gomez's brother or Morticia's uncle (or both)
9. Paul McCartney song lyric: "We're so sorry, _____"
10. Spun tales of Br'er Rabbit and sang "Zip-A-Dee-Doo-Dah"
11. The other nickname for "Mr. Television"
12. Accidentally handed Mr. Potter $8,000 of the Building and Loan's money

SEE THE LIGHT

Described below are fifteen pop culture items containing the word <u>light</u> (or its alternative spelling <u>lite</u>). Identify them all.

1. Song containing oft-misquoted line "Revved up like a deuce"
2. Played Angela Bower on *Who's the Boss?*
3. Illuminated colored peg board toy
4. Neil Diamond song about E.T.
5. Michael J. Fox–Joan Jett film
6. Weapon of choice for Jedis
7. Ad slogan: "I believe in _____, cuz I believe in me."
8. They sang "Groove Is in the Heart."
9. Charlie Chaplin falls for a blind flower girl in this classic
10. This show's highlight was when David and Maddie "did it"
11. Great-tasting, less-filling beverage
12. Doors' song covered by Jose Feliciano
13. Creates groovy color effects on fluorescent posters
14. Sang the song "Pure"
15. Smash hit sung by Vicki Lawrence

No Relation

Described below are thirty celebrities. Each celebrity in the left column has the same last name as, but is not a blood relative of, a celebrity in the right column. Match the celebrities with their namesakes.

1. TV's Edith Bunker
2. Sang "Rocky Mountain High"
3. Co-starred with Francis the Talking Mule
4. Star of *The Seventh Sign*
5. Often teamed with Spencer Tracy
6. Sang "Kiss Me Deadly" in 1988
7. Played Norman Bates
8. Tim Burton's Batman
9. Star of *Meatballs*
10. One-time spokesman for Ritz crackers
11. TV's Maxwell Smart
12. The thirty-ninth U.S. President
13. "The Godfather of Soul"
14. His horse was Trigger
15. TV's Potsie

A. Hosted *Mutual of Omaha's Wild Kingdom*
B. Ripped up the Pope's photo on *Saturday Night Live*
C. Star of *Gimme A Break!*
D. Won Best Supporting Actress Oscar in 1981
E. Sang "You Needed Me" and "Snowbird"
F. Starred in *Popeye*
G. Her last film was *Always*
H. Gilligan or Maynard G. Krebs
I. Sang love theme from *Robin Hood: Prince of Thieves*
J. Star of *A Stranger Among Us*
K. Han Solo or Indiana Jones
L. TV's Molly Dodd
M. Played the Saint and James Bond
N. Played Annie Hall
O. Creator of X the Owl and Donkey Hotey

A BARREL OF PRIMATES

Described below are thirteen primate characters from TV and film. Name them all, or be slated for Project X.

1. Longtime resident of Peebles' Pet Store
2. Tarzan's comic relief
3. Ross Geller's pet monkey
4. Spridal Racer's best pal
5. Outacts Clint Eastwood in *Every Which Way But Loose*
6. Companion to Jennifer of the Jungle on *The Electric Company*
7. Infamous co-star of Ronald Reagan
8. Saturday morning Secret Chimp
9. "King of the Apes" in Disney's *The Jungle Book*
10. TV orangutan who became a government consultant
11. Space Ghost's animal helper
12. Roddy McDowell played him in *Planet of the Apes*
13. Mischievous capuchin in *Monkey Trouble*

AN ANATOMY LESSON

Described below are twenty pop culture items that contain names of body parts in them. Identify them all.

1. Top box office grossing film of 1975
2. Roberta Flack song
3. Toucan Sam's advice for finding Froot Loops
4. Love ballad by Journey
5. Jethro Tull album and song
6. Sang "Feed the Tree"
7. Unidentified informant in *All the President's Men*
8. Ad slogan for the Colonel's chicken
9. The Monkees' movie
10. ZZ Top song from *Eliminator*
11. Teacher in *Fast Times at Ridgemont High*
12. Natalie Wood's last movie
13. Hit song by Quarterflash
14. Judd Nelson–Elizabeth Perkins movie
15. Misogynist Rolling Stones song from *Aftermath*
16. Schoolhouse Rock segment about Manifest Destiny
17. "Aquarius/Let the Sunshine In" is from this musical
18. Cheech and Chong comedy skit featuring Alice Bowie
19. Movie about a town that outlaws dancing
20. Nickname for Major Houlihan

ANSWERS

1. *Jaws*
2. "First Time Ever I Saw Your Face"
3. "Follow your nose"
4. "Open Arms"
5. *Aqualung*
6. Belly
7. Deep Throat
8. "Finger Lickin' Good"
9. *Head*
10. "Legs"
11. Mr. Hand
12. *Brainstorm*
13. "Harden My Heart"
14. *From the Hip*
15. "Under My Thumb"
16. "Elbow Room"
17. *Hair*
18. "Earache My Eye"
19. *Footloose*
20. Hot Lips

Kind of a Drag

Answer the following pop culture trivia questions about cross-dressing.

1. Name the movies in which a character cross-dresses in order to:
   a. Get a part in a soap opera
   b. Study the Talmud
   c. Hide from mobsters after St. Valentine's Day massacre
   d. Be his own mother
   e. See and take care of his kids
   f. Become a Parisian lounge act sensation

2. a-f. Now name the actors who donned the garb of the opposite sex in the above-named movies.

3. Name David Johansen's cross-dressing punk band

4. Who was Glenn Milstead better known as?

5. The Kinks and Lou Reed had famous songs about transvestites. Name the songs.

6. Who was Flip Wilson's feminine alter ego?

7. Ed Wood directed an entire film about cross-dressing. Name it.

8. On *Bosom Buddies*, Tom Hanks and Peter Scolari dress in drag to secure a cheap room in a hotel for women. What were the names of their characters, and the respective names of their feminine aliases?

JOHN? YOU HOME?

POP GOES THE WORLD

Described below are fifteen pop culture items with foreign places (i.e., places outside the U.S.) featured in their names. Identify them all.

1. Hit song from the musical *Chess*
2. Sidekick of Secret Squirrel
3. Notorious Madonna–Sean Penn bomb
4. Played Buddy Sorrell on *The Dick Van Dyke Show*
5. Sang "The Metro" and "Take My Breath Away"
6. "Witch doctor" on *Bewitched*
7. Signature Warren Zevon tune
8. Terry Gilliam film with Jonathan Pryce as a beleagured office worker

9. Star of TV's *Medical Center*
10. During the Three Mile Island crisis, this relevant movie was playing in theaters.
11. Their biggest hit was "Heat of the Moment."
12. Product advertised on consecutive highway billboards with rhyming messages
13. Falco's follow-up to "Rock Me Amadeus"
14. Frequent *Sports Illustrated* swimsuit model and star of *Necessary Roughness*
15. Director David Lean's last film